MARIEL AND CUBAN NATIONAL IDENTITY

Dr. Mercedes Cros Sandoval

Mariel and Cuban National Identity

Cover design: Silvio

First edition: May 1986

© 1985: Dr. Mercedes Cros Sandoval

ISBN 0-918901-30-8

Library of Congress Card Number 85-081703

To ESPAÑA, AFRICA, France, Arawak and whatever other ingredients embraced engendering *campechanería*. To them, *campechanas* and *campechanos* wherever they might be, galant outcasts of the impersonal, dehumanizing encroachments of materialism. *La Caridad* always forgiving and the Caribbean ever nourishing await.

En fin, a tío Rigo y a tía Marta —campechanos—, a tío Germán y a tía Lilia, —gallegos—, quienes juntos con mis padres llenaron mi niñez de cariño.

PROLOGUE

Many journalists dread the call of an academician with a request to review an unpublished manuscript. Granted that part of this feeling is caused a bit by envy. Journalists often must write their stories, columns, or editorials in hours, or even minutes, to meet deadline. The luxury of a few days to do a story really well is something few journalists get and all yearn for. The thought that the person whose manuscript you are reading has had the luxury of weeks, or months to research, write, revise, and polish is one that bothers many of us who just prepare opinions by the hour.

Then comes that other prejudice. Journalists write about today, about important things, about events and people who can change the destiny of a city or the world. Many academicians write in the abstract and offer impractical solutions to problems more prevalent in their minds than in the real world.

I must admit that all of these ideas came to mind when Dr. Mercedes Sandoval called a few months ago and asked me to read a manuscript she had written about the Cubans who had come on the 1980 Mariel boatlift. Mercedes told me she just wanted me to read the manuscript and give her my opinion. She insisted that she would not ask me to write a prologue to her work, unless I would volunteer to do it.

With all of these trepidations, I picked up her typewritten manuscript one night with the idea that it would be a chore. I was certain that it would take me several nights to plow through it.

I was wrong, I read Dr. Sandoval's book that same night. Not that it has as much suspense and intrigue as a good mystery novel. It can't. We all know the basic facts about the Mariel boatlift, about how many people came over, about the criminals, about the success stories. We have also had our share of analytical pieces of why Mariel took place and the possibilities of a new boatlift in the future.

Dr. Sandoval's book is different, however, and this is the beauty of it. Because of her background in popular Cuban folklore, Dr. Sandoval was able to put Mariel into perspective and to do so in a manner refreshing and informative to an expert and interesting to a novice.

But Dr. Sandoval's book does more. In many ways the things she writes about give Cubans and non-Cubans alike an inside look into the idiosincrasies of what is to be Cuban. She does this with a soft folksy approach that gives considerable insights to the person unversed in things Cuban. At the same time, Cubans who read her book will often smile with the warmth that comes from a long-forgotten pleasant memory.

Academicians will find that Dr. Sandoval knows her subject well and writes in the language that they speak and understand. The lay reader will find that this book is not only informative but interesting to read.

Perhaps, however, the true value of this book is not for people of this generation. We are too close to the events of which Dr. Sandoval writes to give proper value to her work. Perhaps the full recognition will come in future years when still unborn generations of Americans of Cuban heritage go back to search for the essence of their roots. When they do, one of the book they will have to turn to is the one Dr. Sandoval has written, as she says, much too modestly: "To try to put Mariel in perspective". She has done that and much more. It is a book that should be read by government officials, by students, and teachers who want to understand Cubans, and by those of us who want to better understand who we are and where we came from.

Guillermo Martínez
The Miami Herald

I

INTRODUCTION

On April 4, 1980, the Cuban government removed the guards from the Peruvian Embassy in Havana as a reprisal measure for its liberal granting of asylum to Cuban nationals. A few days before, Peru had granted asylum to six desperados who, using a truck, had broken into Embassy grounds and caused a shooting that resulted in the death of one of the guards and the wounding of three of the individuals in the truck.

The Cuban government announced and disseminated the word of its unusual decision to leave the Peruvian Embassy unguarded, while inviting the dissatisfied to seek refuge, if they wanted to. As this news spread throughout the Island, thousands of Cubans attempted to enter the Embassy grounds. In less than forty-eight hours 10,800 succeeded. This event was interpreted by many observers as the first free election held in Castro's Cuba. "Cubans vote with their feet" (1) reported the international press.

As days passed, the plight and uncertain destiny of the over-crowded and neglected Peruvian Embassy freedom seekers filled the international media, with a resulting barrage of negative publicity for Castro and his regime. While the world reacted to the diplomatic and human crisis caused by this incident, Cubans in Miami rejoiced, with apprehension, at what they perceived as the heroic deed of those, who, exposing themselves to all types of physical and psychological abuse and uncertainty, had so decisively repudiated the communist system —the same system which, in the past, had caused painful uprooting and earlier diasporas. The mood of joyful apprehension of Cubans in Miami continued to escalate, fed by the news of the negative international reaction to Castro's cruelty (2). The government of Costa Rica, Peru, Spain and the United States offered asylum to these unfortunate people. Then Castro, in an impromptu speech, announced that he was opening the northern harbor of Mariel as an embarcation port for the Embassy refugees. It was also to be used by Cuban Americans to pick up relatives who wanted to abandon the island. The stage had been set for the "freedom flotilla".

The United States govenment was taken by surprise and reacted in a hesitant and confused manner (3). Cuban Americans hurried to seek their relatives. They rented and purchased boats, in many instances paid for by the acquisition of second mortgages on their homes or loans obtained from banks, relatives, or friends. In the end, the United States federal government accepted the "de facto" dictation of immigration policy, when President Jimmy Carter stated on May 5, 1980: "We'll continue to provide an open heart and open arms to refugees seeking freedom from Communist domination" (4). This freedom flotilla brought to the United States more than 125,000 unscreened and undocumented aliens during the months of May, June, July, August and September, when Castro abruptly put an end to it.

At first, Dade County's Cuban community was exhilarated by the flotilla. This community had become economically and socially established in a period of less than twenty years. It had gained a reputation as an achievement-oriented and hard-working community with a large middle class of professionals, technicians, managers, etc., and a substantial number of very successful entrepreneurs. Cuban Americans saw Castro's decision as a symptom of weakness and rejoiced at the adverse publicity that the massive exodus had elicited in international circles. They also hoped that this human stampede would cause a backlash among the many dissatisfied people on the Island who had no one to claim them and who would perceive their fate as hopeless.

The Cuban exiled community hailed this generation of freedom seekers as heroes. The fact that many Mariel refugees had been born or reared in Revolutionary Cuba generated enthusiasm among the nostalgic, longing and guilt-ridden exile community. Their economic and overall "success story" had not weakened their nostalgia; nor had it lessened the guilt of having left behind their homeland, relatives, political prisoners, and countrymen in a world of oppression and scarcity. They felt the flotilla exposed to the entire world the failure of Castro's communism. The choice of abandoning the Island in the earlier years of the Revolution had been a wise one, not the cowardly act of *gusanos* (worms) as Castro labeled those who abandoned Cuba.

Feelings of guilt and nostalgia turned into joy as Cuban Americans saw young men, many of Black ancestry, reach U.S.A. shores in search of freedom. The presence of a great number of Blacks among the *Marielitos* (5) shattered Castro's portrayal of Blacks as massively supportive of the Revolution, which according to him, delivered them from the oppression and segregation of pre-Revolutionary times. Joy, however, was short-lived. A few weeks after this Exodus began it became evident that Castro was using the flotilla to relieve the presures on his regime caused by under and unemployment, acute housing shortages and scarcity (6). Discontent was also, in part, due to the visits of Miami-based Cubans to the Island. Through the so called *viajes de la comunidad* (exiled community visits) more than 100,000 visited the Island in 1979. They brought their relatives and friends all kinds of presents and, apparently, an exaggerated account of the affluence and good life they were enjoying in the United States.

Soon it became evident, also, that Castro, who had characterized the Peruvian Embassy refugees as *escoria* (scum), was packing the boats with people he picked from the streets (prostitutes, homosexuals, and pimps) (7), from hospitals (mentally ill and terminal patients), and from prisons (unwanted criminals and felons). Castro was including these antisocial people in the boatlift to discredit the Peruvian Embassy crowds, to embarass and threaten the exiled Cuban community, and also to defy the government of the United States with this unprecedent act of disrespect for international law and order. As joyful Cuban Americans arrived in Mariel to claim their relatives, hopes were shattered, when, in most instances, only some of those claimed were allowed to leave the Island (8). Instead, their boats were filled with strangers and *escoria*. Meanwhile, Dade County braced itself to accommodate, as well as possible, the influx of the wanted, not so wanted and unwanted stream of refugees.

Shock, repulsion, distance and disengagement began to emerge among established exiles, prompted not only by the presence of these antisocial elements in the flotilla, but also by the demanding, ungrateful and inconsiderate demeanor exhibited by some of them. Over and over again the phrases were repeated: "These people are not like us. They look different. They act different. They are not Cubans as we know Cubans to be. They think they deserve all the help we have given them and more." Cuban Americans were experiencing difficulty accepting these Cubans whose adaptive strategies were so different from theirs. Distance was being introduced by the conflict of values experienced between some of the *Marielitos* and Dade County Cubans, specifically in reference to self discipline, attitudes toward privacy, work and money, and life expectations. These differences were due to the disparate paths followed by the two Cuban groups while accommodating to the pressures of two distinct materialistic ideologies: American capitalism and free enterprise graced by seemingly boundless material resources on the one hand and Castro's brand of tropical communism plagued by scarcity, inconsistency, and oppression on the other. Cuban Americans inwardly blamed the *Marielitos* for shattering the romantic ideal and nostalgic view they had so arduously preserved of Cuba and Cubans. Repulsion was also heightened by the crime wave which swept Dade County and in which the *Marielitos* actively participated. This caused loss of face and damaging backlash to the Cuban American community in Dade County and throughout the United States(9).

In spite of it all, however, the community demonstrated the ability to help absorb the majority of the newly arrived, while watching apprehensively as some made their way to the cemetery or prison.

A. Identification of the Problem

Now, in 1986, six years after the initial shock, as Dade County is reinstating its pre-Mariel image, and a majority of the *Marielitos* have succeded in assimilating, the time has come to reflect upon the Mariel influx. The time has come to assess the *Marielitos* —who they really were, are now, and what they represented; also, to evaluate the information they brought about life in Cuba that is so painfully intertwined with their experiences. It is time to analyze the great stressors and losses which prompted their unusual and not so unusual coping mechanisms. Even further, the time has come to assess the ability of the communist regime to incorporate ideologically and otherwise, great segments of the population of the Island to the essence and goals of revolutionary life. It is time to evaluate whether or not the Revolution has been capable of triggering a syncretic process which blends the attitudes and values of the former Cuban culture with alien, imported ideologies —a syncretic process which, theoretically, could ensure the emergence of a comprehensive all embracing national identity with which a majority of the Cuban people could identify and not just endure.

II

DATA BASE

At the time the Mariel boatlift took place, the author was the director of the Cuban and Puerto Rican Units of Catchment Area IV Community Mental Health Program, these units were located in the Allapattah and Wynwood neighborhoods of Miami, both of which functioned as buffer zones between the Cuban community to the South and the Black communtiy to the North. Most of the residents of these neighborhoods are of lower middle and lower socioeconomic status. The Cuban and Puerto Rican outpatient units rendered services to over six hundred unduplicated clients each month. Most of the clients were of Cuban and Puerto Rican background with significant numbers of Central Americans, Black and White Americans. Approximately 50% of the clients were individuals who had been released from mental hospitals and needed after-care services such as medication, support, therapy, day care services, etc. The remaining 50% of the clients were individuals who had no previous clinical history but who were suffering from the problems caused by culture shock; i.e., identity crisis, role ambiguity, psychological ambivalence, feelings of loss, lack of control, etc. They were people experiencing coping problems while attempting to incorporate themselves into mainstream American society.

When the boatlift started, a great number of our Cuban clients experienced anxiety and depression due to the pressures caused by their need to raise money to rent boats to pick up their relatives in Cuba. Later, when their relatives arrived these clients began manifesting frustration, anxiety and depression —caused, this time, by the problems they were having in accepting and being accepted by the newly arrived.

Our clients resented and complained about the *Marielitos* whom they perceived as irresponsible, inconsiderate, ungrateful and too demanding. They said the *Marielitos* thought they deserved everything because of the suffering they had experienced under communist rule. They claimed the *Marielitos* were incapable of thanking others and appreciating the great sacrifice many Miami Cubans had made in order to bring them to the U.S.A. Our clients maintained that the *Marielitos* were lazy, unappreciative of the value of money, had no desire to work, didn't know how to do anything, and were suspicious of everybody. They thought that the *Marielitos* had unrealistic expectations, hoping to gain higher salaries than their skills would warrant; and feeling that they were taken advantage of if salaries were not in line with their expectations. On the other hand, *Marielitos* complainded that Miami Cubans were very materialistic, thought only about working, were too self sufficient, and, while visiting the Island, had exaggerated the riches they enjoyed in Miami. This stimulated the imagination of Cubans on the Island toward very unrealistic expectations.

The author began interviewing clients and their newly arrived relatives to obtain a better understanding of the situation. The Cuban Mental Health Unit developed clients' support groups to help them deal more effectively with their relatives. *Marielitos* were interviewed, as available, in their relatives' homes, in parks, on street corners, at tent city (10), in hotels, etc. Subsequently, the Mental Health Unit began administering a questionnaire designed to gather information concerning the extent of alcoholism among the newly arrived, as well as their attitudes toward the Miami police and toward freedom.

Federal aid arrived to help Dade County deal with the problems brought about by the refugee influx. At that time, the Community Mental Health Center received funds to develop specific programs for the Mariel and Haitian entrants. The author, then Director of Hispanic Services, was in charge of the two above-mentioned outpatient units and of developing a special program for *Marielitos* consisting of an outpatient component, transitional living arrangements and day care services. Many of the staff recruited for the delivery of these services were Mariel refugees. Among them were three psychiatrists, four fifth-year medical students, a vocational psychologist, a nurse and a chauffeur.

Hispanic Services provided outpatient care to over seven hundred and fifty unduplicated *Marielitos*. The great majority of the services were rendered to clients with no previous psychiatric history. They were people who were experiencing culture shock and were in need of informational and referral services, vocational guidance and general support. Other clients had sought psychiatric aid in Cuba to avoid government regulations which they considered reckless, unfair or ungratifying (i.e., conscription into the Armed Forces, missions to Africa, strenuous labor in rural areas, etc.). Psychiatric aid in Cuba, as reported by Mariel clients and Mariel mental health staff alike, is used for protection from the system and to obtain sedatives.

A psychiatric record does not elicit the stigma with which it is associated in the United States. Some of the clients, however, did have a history of chronicity and had been hospitalized just priors to departure a few months earlier. These clients were offered medication maintenance; therapy, day treatment and, when eligible, transitional living arrangements.

During the period between May, 1980 and March, 1982, the author informally interviewed 439 Cuban Entrants. The interviewes were structured as need assessments to be considered in program development. They were also designed to identify the most prevalent coping patterns achieved by these people while adapting to conditions on the Island. Such information was of importance in developing strategies to facilitate their prompt assimilation into life in Dade County. In addition, it was extremely informative to observe in staff meetings and case presentations the conflict which occurred between the Miami and the Mariel staff. Such conflicts were related to salient differences of opinions regarding clients clinical assessment and recommended therapeutic approaches. These differences were indicative of colflicting worldviews, treatment goals and objectives that were held by mental health professionals of different cultural backgrounds (11).

The following is a breakdown of the sample of 439 individuals interviewed:

Professionals	71	16.1%
Students	69	15.7%
Clerical	24	4.4%
Farmers	6	1.3%
Skilled or Semi-skilled laborers	269	61.2%

These informal interviews were the basis for construction of an interview guide designed to elicit expectations, family configuration, support system, daily routine stressors, etc. This guide was used with 66 informants, allowing collection of data on specified topics and also exploration of other questions in an effort to obtain information about deeply ingrained value orientations, behavioral patterning and basic personality structure.

The following is a breakdown of the sample of 66 informants, allowing collection of data on specified topics and also responding to the interview guide:

Profesionals . . . . 14 . . . . .21.1%
Students . . . . 17 .25.7%
Skilled or
Semi-skilled laborers . . . . 26 .39.3%
Housewives . . . . 2 . . . . 3.0%
Farmers . . . . 2 . . . . 3.0%

The average interview lasted for two to three hours; some longer, according to the willingness of the informant and his communication skills. During the period correspondind to the last five months of 1983 and the first month of 1984, many of the earlier key informants were reinterviewed (12) to determine whether or not the information given had changed and, if so, why. New informants who had come via Mariel (primarily college students) were also interviewed to see if their views were consistent with the data gathered before about life in Cuba versus life in the United States. Confrontation groups were held with these students to assess, in the presence of their peers, the validity of the information given. It became apparent that their observations were sharper and more precise than those of earlier informants and that their views of Cuban Americans and life in the United States were more positive, while their views of life in Cuba were even more negative than those of the earlier informants.

III

WHO ARE THE MARIELITOS

A Statistical Appraisal

The U.S. Department of State official records indicate that 124,779 persons were boatlifted from Cuba during the period of April to October, 1980. Despite the negative image portrayed by the Cuban official media, and, in some instances echoed by the international and American press, the majority of *Marielitos* must be considered as fairly representative of present Cuban society. Dr. Robert Bach (13), who analyzed data collected by the U.S. Immigration Service, describes them as follows, "The arrivals were neither the upper crust nor the bottom layer of Cuban society. They generally possess education and skill levels above the average for those remaining on the Island and about the same as those who arrived in the 1970's." However, there are some important differences in socio-economic background between this group and those who migrated in the 1960's. According to Dr. Juan M. Clark (14) the *Marielitos* share similar characteristics with those Cubans who came to the United States after 1974. He illustrates the differences between the two groups in the following chart (15).

Exiles 1959-1974[a]		Percentage	Mariel-Exodus[b]
Professional, semi-professional managerial	22.2	7.1	Professional
		1.5	Managerial
Sales & clerical	27.8	1.0	Sales
		6.1	Clerial
Services	8.7	10.2	Services
Skilled, semi-skilled, unskilled	35.3	22.7	Craftsmen
		14.1	Machine Operator
		11.2	Transporte Operator
		25.0	Laborer
Extractive: agricultural, mining	6.0	1.1	Extractive Agricultural

Sources:

a. Juan M. Clark, *The Exodus from Revolutionary Cuba (1959-1974) A. Sociological Analysis.* Ph D. Dissertation, University of Florida, 1975.

b. Brookings Institution Sample of 732 refugees at Eglin AFB, directed by Dr. Robert Bach. See, by that author, "The New Cuban Immigrants: their Background and Prospects". *Monthly Labor Review,* October, 1980.

Dr. Clark points out the continuation of an occupational trend started in the latter part of the 1970's. There is a significant increase of blue collar workers and a decrease in the proportion of the professional managerial class in the Mariel population. Clark also makes a reference to the reversal of former trends in sex composition. Among the Mariel refugees males represent 70.2%, while in the previous exodus males represented only 42.1%. The age category also dramatically changed. The median age for Mariel entrants was younger than the previous arrivals; 68.5% were below 36 years of age. Yet, there was a decrease in the number of individuals under 18 years, which, in the Mariel group, was only 20.1%; while among previous arrivals it was 33.5% There was a larger percentage of single individuals; 33.7% versus 5% in the former group. There was also a larger proportion of divorcees; 10.7% versus 5% in earlier waves of immigration, suggesting a higher rate of disintegration of the present Cuban family.

According to Clark's estimates, non-whites constituted from 20-40% of the Mariel group. This trend was new, since non-white Cubans had been highly underrepresented in the past, because of governmental measures designed to prevent non-whites from abandoning the island.

The great majority, 89.2% of Mariel refugees, had some relatives or friends in the U.S.A.; while 28.5% had immediate family in this country. According to the Lasaga survey reported by Clark, only 39% of the respondents were actually picked up by relatives; while 61% either came on their own initiative or were forced to leave by Castro's regime. Clark also reports that 20% of the surveyed refugees had to leave their spouses, because the government did not allow them to come.

The Mariel refugees' prison record, as mentioned earlier, is not as negative as portrayed by Castro and voiced by the press. According to Immigration and Naturalization Service figures quoted by Clark, a total of only 1,761 persons (representing 1.4% of the new immigrants) were classified as felons (convict ed of murder, burglary, rape). an additional 23,927 or 19.1% of the arrivals were placed by the Immigration and Naturalization Service into the combined categories of non-felonous criminals and political prisoners. According to Clark only 2,000 should fall into this category. The problem stems from a question regarding the meaning of a prison record in Cuba. Both Bach and Clark point out that Cuban law categorizes as criminal, activities that in the U.S. are perfectly legitimate, such as buying and selling food and clothing from private salesmen, refusing to do "volunteer" work or agricultural labor, vagrancy, and attempts to leave the island.

Dr. Bach's (16) appraisal of the refugees, based on their socioeconomic background, was that the majority of these refugees would find self-sustaining employment within a relatively short period of time, within the Cuban American working class. This has indeed, been the case.

B. The Marielitos, An Attitudinal Appraisal.

The *Marielitos* may also be classified according to the reasons which prompted their coming to the United States, their willingness to be here and their potential to become adapted to the new milieu.

1. *Los Rezagados* (those left behind). This category represents individuals who were claimed by Miami relatives. They were people who had never accepted the Revolution and who, for various reasons (children, military duty, imprisonment, etc.), had not been able to leave the Island previously. A nineteen year old male student serves as an example of this group:

> I was nineteen when the Mariel boatlift started. Even though I was born during the Revolution my parents always confided to me their rejection of it. They brought me up as a Catholic. I always knew I didn't fit there. I, of course, acted out my role and never got myself in trouble. Most people didn't know how my family and I felt, even though we went to Church on occasions. One day at school the teacher was urging us to join a Domingo Rojo (Red Sunday) and do extra volunteer work in memory of Marx and Lenin. I still don't know why I told the teacher: "Why should I do any-

thing for them? They are gone. You told us we humans are only matter. If that is the case, they are disintegrated matter. Their spirits don't exist. Why should I honor them?" I was very lucky, because the teacher took me aside and said: "Are you crazy? Are you going to argue with the Revolution? Please keep quiet. You are too young to rot in jail." I realized it all, nodded, asked to go to the bathroom, and cried.

2. *Los Desencantados* (the disenchanted). This category includes individuals who were willing actors in the revolutionary experience but had become disenchanted either because they lost its favor or because they felt that the Revolution had failed to fulfill its early promises of progress, freedom and equality. The comments of a twenty-one-year-old female student are illustrative:

I was raised by the Revolution. My dad was a member of the communist Party. We lived well in a nice home in Havana with car and chauffeur. My father always bought me nice Italian shoes and clothes. My sister, my mother and I never lacked anything. Then he died, and we lost all our privileges, and then we had to fare like the rest of the people. At that time I met my husband who was a *gusano* (worm, antirevolutionary Cuban), and when his family claimed him I came.

A forty-five-year-old technician's recollection reflects a similar disenchantment:

At first and for a few years I worked enthusiastically for the Revolution. I went to rallies, joined mass organizations, did volunteer work. When things turned badly I said to myself and others, "These are only mistakes which will be mended with time." So, year after year, I kept my eyes and ears closed and hailed the Revolution. Sometimes, when alone in the bathroon, I was shocked to find myself cursing the Revolution. I used to get scared of myself. Then came *la comunidad* (the Cuban exiled commmunity visits) and with it my brother whom I had not seen in ten years. My brother was younger and less skilled, while I felt old, worn out and sour. Then, I wondered whether it was all worthwhile, whether Castro's people knew what they were doing, whether they were liars using us for their glory and power. When my chance came I did not hesitate, I went into the Embassy.

Some of the members of *los desencantados* were very confused. After all, they had accepted the Revolution and had actively and willingly collaborated in it. Some were suffering from ideological conflict, since their disenchantment with the Revolution was more pragmatic than moral. They reflected a lot of ambivalence mixed with guilt and anger. Of all those abandoning the island, *los desencantados* were the primary target of the Cuban system's rage. They received all types of abuse from the incited mobs (17).

A sixteen-year-old male student gives an account of the beating to death by his own students of a teacher who announced his intentions to leave the island:

> The word was that the teacher, Mr. G., had been claimed by his relatives and was leaving. Everywhere the leaders of the communist youth and some teachers started calling him a traitor and urged the students to make an example of him. We, the students, were afraid, but in Cuba people don't think; you do what you are told to be safe. The students had been told that he had to come back to school a last time. When he came, the inciters started saying: "Let us teach these traitors a message, let us show them how the Revolution takes care of traitors and *vende-patrias* (people who would sell their own homeland)." People started kicking him down the streets for several blocks until he died.

3. **Los Embullados** (those who are carried away by the group or by a mood). This category includes people who were neither partial to nor against the Revolution. However, like the *desencantados* they were blinded by the apparent affluence and well-being of the Cuban Americans who visited Cuba during *los viajes de la comunidad* (exiled community visits to Cuba). For some, having been exposed to the contrast, having gained access to a new point of reference, these visits brought an awareness that life in Cuba is like "rotting alive." Thus, when the possibility arrived of entering the Embassy, coming on a boat, or even obtaining an exit permit by self-accusation of sexual or other social deviations, they took the opportunity and came. They were part of the "fever of enthusiasm" generated in Cuba by the exiled community visits to Cuba and by Mariel. They left Cuba beause they had nothing to lose. In general, however, a great majority of those interviewed, at one point or another, commented that their life in Cuba was so pointless that when their chance to leave arrived, they just took it.

A fifty-two year old female clerk typist remarks as follows:
Life in Havana is a drag. There is nothing pleasant to do but
pasar trabajo (experience every act as a struggle); waiting for
a bus, waiting in lines, trying to hussle for this and the other.
Then my cousin visited from Miami and brought fine presents to me —things that I had forgotten even existed. I was
thankful but a little bit envious; I felt I needed something
more in my life to make it pleasant and worthwhile. Later,
when the boatlift started and my mother told me that my
cousin had sent a boat to get her parents and brother and that
she had also included our names on the list, I did not hesitate.
I was part of the fever that swept Cuba. I left my mother
behind, who was not able to leave because my brother was
comprometido (compromised) by the Revolution. I just
wanted to have something to live for. I did not think that in
Miami I would miss my mother and my brother's family,
that I might face problems getting a job; I just wanted to flee
out of the rot.

Another nineteen year old female student recalls:
My parents, my brother and I lived in the same house with
my uncle, his wife and three children. My uncle's family were
comecandelas (fire eaters), a term used for people who are
unconditionally committed to the Revolution. My uncle and
his son were Party card-carriers. Then my aunt came from
Miami to visit our grandmother, and she brought my oldest
cousin a jacket. He did not go to see my aunt at my grandmother's house, but she sent it to him anyway. When early in
the evening he came home and saw the jacket he said: "What
is this?" "A present from your aunt," I said. "I don't want it,"
he screamed and went into his bedroom. Late that night I
heard him crying and screaming, "this is all shit, all a big lie.
They have lied to me." He was one of the men who entered
the Peruvian Embassy; he left everybody behind...

A fifty year old female informant confides the following:
My ex-husband's family are all communists. I never could
accept the Revolution. Even though my husband was not a
hardline communist, marital problems were caused by the
ideological clash. We had two children who enjoyed many of
the privileges of the new class. One of them visited East
Europe, and everytime my husband or his family traveled

abroad, they brought them good presents, and clothes and shoes. My children were well aware of the feelings I had against the Revolution. The oldest one, however, was very close to his father and his father's family. Then, my sister came to visit from Miami and brought a huge bag with all types of clothing for my children and me. That day was like twenty years of Christmas in one day. That night I heard my oldest son arguing with my husband: "You dirty bastard, you had nice clothes and a nice life when you were young. You are denying this to me because of the power and glory of your Revolution." Two years later, when the Peruvian Embassy incident occurred, my son and his wife (a young woman whose family was integrated into the Revolution) walked into the Embassy. When I found out, my youngest son and I followed.

4. **Los Secuestrados** (the kidnapped ones). This category includes people forced into the boats by Castro's regime. Many of these people never dreamed of coming to Miami and had no relatives in the United States. For example, a thirty-eight year old male of peasant background recounts:

I lived on the farm that used to be my grandfather's with my wife, my three children, my brother's family and my father and mother. I fished for a living and helped the others with farm work. Four years before Mariel I was sentenced for having killed a calf. They gave me ten years, but after two years they let me go because of good behavior while in prison. A few days before Mariel I had killed a pig. One night they came for me and took me to the police station. There, they told me: "We are going to be nice to you. We are going to fulfill your golden dream." "What is that?" I asked. They told me, "Do you want to go to prison or to Miami?" "To Miami," I said. Since I lived near Mariel, a few hours later I was in the boat heading towards Miami, leaving all my life behind, since neither my wife nor children were even told where I was being sent.

This informant was picked up by members of the Mental Health Unit's staff in the yard of San Juan Bosco Church where he had been sleeping for several nights. He had been in Miami for over a year and had had no news of his family, possibly because he had no return address or because they were afraid of writing back to him. He was totally disoriented at the time we picked him up, completely paranoid and delusional. The staff provided him with food and clothing and found him a place to sleep. After several weeks of treatment he became stabilized and related his story to the author. This man had never had any history of mental illness in Cuba, but he had been arrested and kidnapped for having dared to kill a pig raised on the farm of his grandfather, a farm which no one could make him understand was no longer his own. We encouraged him to write to his wife and use the clinic's return address. He did, but she did not reply.

An older lady in her sixties who had been referred to the Clinic asked when leaving: "Where is the stop for the bus that goes to Marianao (a town in Cuba)?" That lady had been taken from a mental hospital and placed on the boat (18).

5. **La Escoria** (the scum). This category includes convicted felons, prostitutes, pimps, and husslers of all types who were picked up in prisons and from the streets and shipped into Miami. Among them were great numbers of hardcore antisocial individuals. Many of them were instrumental in unleashing a homicide wave in Miami when rival jail gangs carried out their vengeances against each other.

Most of the residents of the mental health program's transitional living quarters, which we set up for Mariel refugees, had been in jail. Most of these individuals exhibited the typical behavior of the jail culture: undisciplined, resentful, highly aggressive (verbally and physically), manipulators, perennial thieves, etc. Such individuals were very visible during the first year following the flotilla. Some of them still live marginal lives in the inner city or have made their way to prison.

Many of the residents in the transitional living quarters of the New Horizons Community Mental Health Program told us that Cuban authorities had put it to them in a simple manner: "Do you want to stay in prison some extra years or go to Maimi?" Others who had been freed were asked: "Do you want to go back to jail or to Miami?"

IV

SURVIVAL IN CUBA

During the past twenty-five years life in Cuba has changed markedly because of the imposition of a totalitarian system alien to the traditional values of the people. This system uses physical and psychological measures of coercion to control every move of each resident of the island. The control is so thorough that it leaves no aspect in the life of the individual unturned or unchecked by some government institution or organization. It has such an impact on the individual that, as reported to the author and to Clark (19), people became the ever-watchful censors and repressors of their own behavior.

The ideological pillar of this system is the Cuban Communist Party, which is in charge of the dogmatic enunciation and interpretation of all accepted ideology. As in other communist societies, the party line is the dogmatic foundation of revolutionary indoctrination, educational philosophy, historical accounting, news interpretation and dissemination, artistic expression, athletic participation and even the explanation of the very meaning of existence. Life, acording to official Cuba, has meaning in terms of revolutionary ideology. The Cuban communist Party is the only legal political party. It controls all of the political activities of the island. Along the lines of Russian communism, it is a highly elitist party with a narrow apex of power under Castro. Membership in the Party is an honor which bestows all types of privileges and opportunities.

The communist regime also depends upon a number of institutions and organizations which are directly involved in represive activities. The state police *Seguridad del Estado* (State Security) responds directly to Castro and is in charge of his personal security. State Security has access to information concerning any individual's life, including personal informa tion and even psychiatric reports. The thoroughness of its investigative methods is matched only by the infamous repressive measures it utilizes with individuals considered dangerous to the system. Repression includes all types of psychological horror (arrest without cause, harrassment, false executions), as well as physical abuse and torture (incarceration in small cells exposed to either excessive heat or cold).

La Dirección General de Inteligencia (General Intelligence Directorship). This agency is in charge of espionage and counter espionage activities and also of monitoring every move made by Cubans who travel abroad on athletic, technical, artistic or other missions.

Los Comites de Defensa de la Revolución (Committees for the Defense of the Revolution). These committees exist in each neighborhood, and there is one assigned to each block. They are in charge of organizing volunteer work such as street cleaning, assemblies, blood drives, preventive vaccinations, etc. Aside from this community work, they are in charge of local propaganda, organizing mass mobilization for political rallies, and of patrolling their own block. They are empowered to search any house, bag, package, or individual, if, for any reason, they believe that some illegal activities might be taking place (black marketeering, counterrevolutionary behavior, and the like). They are also in charge of clearing individuals and granting character references for offical documents, promotions, etc. These committees, as an informant stated, "are the eyes of the Revolution at your front door."

Thus, the system has created an institutionalized state of crisis, uncertainty, uprooting, loss, separation, terror, and culture shock which has resulted in the shattering of some of the core institutions and values of the former Cuban culture, while precariously debilitating others. This has caused prevalent feelings of lack of control, desperation, alienation, and hopelessness in large segments of the population.

To survive in Cuba, in order to satisfy the minimal basic needs, one has to engage in certain strategic accommodations: (A) being in the system, (B) resolving problems outside of the system, and (C) protecting oneself from the system.

A. In the System

Since Castro's Cuba is a totalitarian society under the rule of one man, where one political party is allowed, with a sole employer, supplier, educator, healer and political voice (20), every person has a need to be somehow *in* the system. The government "controls all levels of human activity, including the economy, arts, religion and recreation (21)." Under such conditions the government is the only supplier of all the essential goods and services needed to survive.

1. Living Conditions. Living conditions in Cuba are very meager. Per capita income figures place Cuba deep down among the Third World nations. The World Bank ranks Cuba as a "lower middle income" nation, 68th out of 125 countries in the world, with about $1,000 a year income per person (22). Although income distribution is more equitable than before the Revolution, as late as 1973 the wealthiest 10% earned approximately 100 times more than the poorest 10%. Mismanagement and the use of resources to subsidize an armaments race and revolutionary adventures overseas are the apparent reasons for the meager conditions of the Cuban consumer. However, very few Cubans, if any, are completely destitute, and health care and education are free (23).

Living conditions are deplorable in most instances. The housing shortage is so accute that overcrowding, slum conditions and the deterioration of existing housing units is rampant. The government policies have made Cuba a country of homeowners (78% of the population), and those who rent pay only 10% of their salary for a period of twenty years, when the property is given to them. However, the scarcity of housing and the conditions of existing ones are deplorable.

According to Recarte (24), at the end of the 1950's it was estimated that 28,000 homes and apartments had to be built annually to satisfy the increasing population needs. In 1975 Castro announced that, after fifteen years in power, the average number of new homes/ apartments built was 12,500 a year. Thus, the housing deficit is endemic in spite of the hundreds of thousands of Cubans who abandoned their homes to the government when fleeing the island, a process encouraged by the government which, in many instances, facilitated the exit of home owners in order to take over all of their possessions (25).

This housing deficit results in the constant subdivision of existing units; for example, to make room for a newlywed daughter or son who cannot get living quarters elsewhere. Frequently, divorced people have to remain in the same dwelling, because there is no place for them to go. Housing shortages have also caused the endemic growth of large slum areas inside of and around practically every town and city (26). Since construction materials are not available, houses go unrepaired for years, a practice which contributes to further deterioration. The new units built by the government deteriorate very quickly because of the poor quality of materials used in their construction (27).

Essential utility services are also very poor. Blackouts are part of daily life; they occur practically everyday. In most instances the government announces in advance the areas which are going to be affected to enable people to take necessary precautions. Selective neighborhoods where the elite of government officials and foreign dignitaries live, are not affected by these constant blackouts. Water shortage is also endemic (28), as is the scarcity of essential fuels like kerosene, gasoline, and charcoal.

Transportation in Cuba is difficult. Almost everyone relies on public busses which are in poor condition, overcrowded and late. Only the elite have access to private cars, normally Fiats, Volkswagens, Lada Skenas, Meskovich Renaults, and Toyotas. Some relics of the 1950's are still used by those lucky owners who struggle to keep them going, relying on Cuba's mechanical ingenuity to build spare parts. An old car in Cuba may sell for 10,000 *pesos* (Cuban dollars).

2. The Ration Book. The Ration Book or *Libreta de Abastecimiento* is the official door to government run stores where the individual can get, when available, and at a reasonable price, those items assigned to him by government regulation, which are always in restricted quantity and of dubious quality (29). The amounts of items vary, but normally a Ration Book entitles the owner to purchase each month from two to four pounds of rice (the quantity fluctuating according to availability), four pounds of sugar, one-and-a-half pounds of lard and fourteen ounces of beans. Each person is entitled to purchase three-forths of a pound of meat every eleven days and two pounds of chicken every fifteen days (30). It often happens that, after spending four or five hours in a line in front of the store to buy a product one is entitled to, the product has been sold out when one's turn comes. On occasions a particular item might be placed *por la libre,* which means that one can buy as much as is desired. These situations force the consumer to be always on the lookout in order to obtain a minimal supply of goods.

Since 1979 the government has also created a "parallel market," opening some stores where one can purchase any item free of restrictions but five times more expensive than the rationed counterpart. The parallel market has been dubbed the "Red Market," since it is the government's controlled black market.

3. Education. Elementary and basic secondary education up to the ninth grade is free and mandatory. After graduating from basic secondary education the individual has two options: to quit studying altogether, which might entail being unemployed for several years, or to opt for either technical education or pre-university programs.

Pre-university studies comprise grades 10, 11, 12 and 13. Good grades and good revolutionary behavior and attitudes are the criteria for admission. After concluding pre-university studies one applies to the University, identifying five career choices. Chances are that one will be admitted to the University but not to the career of first choice.

Some career choices (such as Economics, Law, Humanities, and International Law, as well as scholarships to study in East European countries), are restricted to students with proved revolutionary militancy. Law studies were reinstituted in the mid-1970's. Before that, the government had deemed it unnecessary to have lawyers in a socialistic society. Admission to the School of Medicine varies according to international demand and government expediency. The Cuban government loans physicians to some Third World nations who pay a salary in dollars ($) to the Cuban government, which pockets it while paying the physicians a meager salary in *pesos*.

Many youngsters receive scholarships (including room and board) when entering basic secondary studies but some, even while in elementary school. Most of these *becados* (scholarship recipients) are sent to country schools where they have a strict schedule, devoting four hours a day to the classroom, four to agricultural activities and three hours in the evening to homework.

Those who go to school in the city or towns also have to provide volunteer agricultural labor for either forty-five days or three months a year in a program which starts in basic secondary school. Many of my young informants complained that there was poor supervision during their stay in the countryside and that, in some instances, girls and boys were housed in the same quarters with rampant sexual experimentation involving, also, very young unprepared teachers who were assigned to them.

In general, the interviewees expressed a conviction that education in Cuba was sound, that there was a lot of motivation to study, and that there were pressures to do so (31). Some complained that a shortage of teachers sometimes resulted in the use of very young, poorly trained student-teachers as instructors, but, in general, they felt that education was good. A twenty-three year old male student recalls, for example:

> I was in 12th grade (1973-74) at V.I. Lenin Vocational
> School, a Castro showcase, in Havana. I was a student
> assistant of the Spanish course when I was approached by the
> 12th. grade coordinator and asked to teach the course I was
> taking. I had to receive an intensive seminar on Spanish
> Grammar (which was the content of that Junior High School
> course), because I was hardly familiar with the subject. I did it
> because I liked the idea, since this new task would release me
> from my four hours of work at the school plantation.

Many of the interviewees complained of the thorough indoctrination which permeates the educational process, with Marxist Leninism being taught in a dogmatic fashion with no room for reflection or discussion. By way of example, the informant mentioned directly above recalls the case of Carmen, a Spanish student of architecture at Havana University.

> She was, at that time (1979-80) member of the Spanish
> Communist Party (which follows Carrillo's Eurocommu-
> nism line, as opposed to the Cuban Communist Party which
> follows Moscow's line). She was always in trouble in the
> Marxism class, to the point that it was evident she would fail.
> One day she stood in front of the class and told the professor
> that, following instructions from her party, she would not
> make more comments. At the end of the Fall term, the
> Architecture Department published the list with the name
> and GPA of the 5th year students. According to the GPA
> rank, the students are allowed to choose their graduation
> thesis. It happened that the UIA (International Union of
> Architects) called for the student contest to be held in Mexico
> by mid-year (1980). As had been customary, the student with
> the best GPA is awarded the right to enter the contest.
> Carmen had the highest GPA, but was not allowed to choose
> a graduation thesis, or enter the contest project. It was
> offered, intead, to the student that was in charge of the UJC
> (Young Communist League)."

A nineteen year old female informant related the following:

> "Even though as a child I had very few opportunities to eat
> lobster or shrimp. they were my favorite food. One day, when
> I was fourteen, I was reading a book on Cuba's natural
> resources, which mentioned the abundance of crustaceans in

Cuba's submarine platform. That day in class I asked the teacher why it was that in Cuba crustaceans were not available for consumption. The classroom suddenly went silent. The teacher, obviously in distress, hesitated, as if taken by surprise, and later explained that the reason was that Cuba needed the income generated by the sale of lobsters and shrimp to pay for industrial equipment and to aid the other underdeveloped nations of the world. When the class was over, the teacher, who was very fond of me, called me and said: "Please, María why do you ask such silly and dangerous questions? Don't you know any better? Don't be foolish and don't ever ask any questions which could embarass the government unless you want to get in big trouble."

The *Federación de Estudiantes Universitarios* (Federation of University Students), which in pre-revolutionary times engaged in all types of political activities tinged with all colors of ideology, and, in most instances, led opposition and confrontation struggles against the government, is now used by the regime to control and oversee student activities, assure that the official propaganda is disseminated and secure student participation in mass rallies.

In several group discussions that I conducted with Miami students aged 18-22 years, in both 1981 and 1984, the Mariel participants bitterly complained of the effects indoctrination had on them, the fact that history was continuously used to suit revolutionary dogma, and the way events were misconstrued to create antagonistic feelings against the West, etc. The most interesting comments related to the United States being depicted as a place where Blacks are perennially chased by dogs (32) and where Cubans are discriminated against. According to Marielito students in Miami, this propaganda alienates the students. As one puts it: "Cuba is like the planet Uranus, a place where we only get whatever information they allow and as interpreted by them."

This feature of the Cuban educational system makes it very vulnerable, since any contact with the outside world will clearly demonstrate the frequent lies and distortions of the truth used by the government to preserve revolutionary loyalty. If, in spite of massive propaganda, 11,000 Cubans walked into the Peruvian Embassy and thousands applied for visas to the United States, the implication is that, either people don't believe what they are told, or they would rather be segregated in the United States than be in their own homeland (33).

4. Employment. Since the government is practically the sole employer, Cubans are forced to work in the system and to abide by the many regulations and restrictions that this entails. Workers in factories are pressured to join the *Comités Obreros* (Workmen Committees) if they want to enjoy the meager opportunities for advancement that are available and to avoid undesirable shifts, transfers, or schedules.

The communist system in Cuba has used former mass organizations and has created new ones as instruments of controlling the lives of individuals. Labor unions, which, in the past, represented the interests of its members, have been turned into their censors and overseers. The labor unions are used to make propaganda for the system, to encourage volunteer work and donations and to elicit greater productivity from the workers they are supposed to represent. They are also used to organize mass participation in political rallies, meetings, etc.

Women have been pressured to join *La Federación de Mujeres Cubanas* (Cuban Women's Federation) which, also, is an organization utilized by the system to disseminate propaganda, to encourage volunteerism and to facilitate mass mobilization.

As described in the above section, Castro's Cuba is a totalitarian society where the government, as sole employer and supplier, also controls the political, academic and social life of the people.
B. Resolving Problems Outside of the System.

Resolver (find solutions to) is the verb used in Cuba to depict the innumerable amount of activities in which the individual has to engage in order to be able to satisfy the most basic needs. Most of these activities are illegal and have to do with dealings in the black market.

1. Black Market. Practically everybody except members of the government elite actively participate in the black market. Conditions in Cuba are such that the system forces everybody to engage in illegal activities. This raises a question regarding the etiology of the sociopathology manifested by some of the Marielitos and the admission by most of them of having engaged in illegal barter, occasional stealing, perennial pretending, lying, and the like. Apparently, the system, either intentionally or unintentionally, is the factor

causing sociopathological behavior in people only striving to survive.
A twenty-three-year-old male informant recounts the following:

> The act of stealing raw materials or finished goods from your
> working place does not have a bad connotation in the eyes of
> the regular Cuban. On the contrary, it is what your family or
> your friends expect you to do! When I was short of
> typewriting paper, and since it was impossible to get it in the
> store, I just went to see my cousin, who was then working as a
> secretary, and she managed to get me paper and other office
> supplies.

It is in the black market that one acquires everything: food,
clothing, drivers licenses, false documentation, electrical appliances,
everything. The informant mentioned above recalls:

> Just months before Mariel, I bought a 1/4" electric drill
> (Hitachi) for $90. Months later in Miami, I went to Sears and
> bought a similar drill for just $10.

It is in the black market that people find solutions. There one
acquires those articles which are not available in the Ration Book or
which cannot be acquired in sufficient quantities by means of the
Ration Book.

Articles sold in the black market are obtained by stealing them
from government warehouses, groceries stores, farms, etc. The
consensus is that "It is O.K. to steal from the government; everybody
does." "Do you think I am going to lack light bulbs in my house if I
can take them from the office?" "Do you think that the daughter of
the butcher is going to go without good clothes if all he has to do is
take some meat and sell it at five times its ration price to a grateful
favored customer?"

The black market is so much a part of Cuba's life that everybody
leaves home with a bag called *la por si acaso* (the just in case bag), just
in case one sees an opportunity to buy or exchange something. A lot
of time and energy are devoted to black-marketeering activities which
are called *el trapicheo* (small trading).

In the small towns and in the countryside it is easier to obtain food,
since eager farmers are ready to exchange produce for clothing
articles which are scarce where they live. In the city, clothing, watches,
appliances, are more readily available, with new supplies coming
from sailors and foreigners who gladly benefit from these activities.

A great part of people's salaries are used for black-marketeering. It
is so vital to their means of existence that, in many instances, people

obtain medical certificates to be able to excuse themselves from their jobs in order to take care of some profitable deal available to them (34).

In such a society a successful person is one who *tiene una busca* (has a contact in the countryside) which will enable him to obtain food products for consumption or for further exchange. Stealing from the government is not only respectable but admirable. Informants say: "Everybody steals in Cuba: the butcher, the store keeper, the farmer; everybody except those high in the government who don't have to steal. Everybody hustles in Cuba in order to survive."

2. Sociolismo. The need to engage in illegal and persecuted activities in Cuba is such that it has given birth to a new type of relationship: *El Sociolismo*. In a joking manner Cubans say that in Cuba there is no such thing as socialism but *sociolismo*, an interpersonal economic and supportive network. *Sociolismo* is a word derived from the Spanish word *socio* meaning partner. *Socio* is the person who helps you solve problems. The butcher who sells you a pound of meat on the black market is your *socio*, a person whom you need and to whom you feel grateful. The storekeeper who sells you panties *por la izquierda* (with the left hand), is also your *socio*, as is the farmer who gives you produce in exchange for your old clothes. Your *socio* is the person who signs your name on an attendance sheet at a revolutionary meeting or punches the clock for you in a factory. The doctor who gives you a medical certificate to excuse you from volunteer work or other hassles is also your *socio*.

Your *socio* is the team leader in charge of a youth group assigned to agricultural labor, who, at the time of reporting the number of buckets of potatoes you picked, will report a few extra. He doesn't need to tell you directly that he protected you, but you know; and when the time comes that he needs your assistance, you return the favor. Your *socio* is the person in charge of a warehouse who sees you stealing oil and will neither report nor say anything to you, but who, possibly, a few days later will ask you to run some errand for him. *Socios* are the persons you need to beat the oppressive and miserly system.

C. Protecting Yourself from the System
1. The Family. The Cuban extended family, which was the nourishing institution of the culture from an economic, social and emotional point of view, has been badly damaged. It has been

practically dissolved by loss, uprooting, distance caused by former emigrations, and distrust due to conflicting political stances. The nuclear family precariously survives with the traditional sex and age roles shattered or abolished (35).

The father-husband role has been dangerously weakened since the man is no longer the provider-head of the family. He has lost control of the members of the family, since he cannot oppose his wife's revolutionary duties or work demands. He has no control over his children's education or whereabouts and can poorly provide for family needs. His authority is second to revolutionary whim and law. His precedence over wife and children has diminished. Even the traditional possessiveness and domination of the *macho* ideal cannot manifest itself in anyting but superfluous manner, perhaps by preventing his wife from wearing certain clothing. Simultaneously, however, he might have to allow her to do guard duty with a neighbor whom he perceives as a threat and a cause for jealousy.

The extreme cult of personality surrounding Castro, which embraces all aspects of Cuban life, leaves little room for even the positive manifestation of *machismo* or *hombre de bien*. Castro's own *machismo*, so propagandized and emphasized, leaves little room for others' manliness.

The traditional role of the Cuban female as mother-wife has also changed dramatically, since most women have been urged to be liberated, to work and join revolutionary organizations. This leaves little time for the nourishing role of the traditional Cuban woman. The endemic scarcity of consumer goods, the lack or domestic privacy caused by overcrowded conditions, the never-ending lines in front of stores, offices, etc., fills domestic life with frustration, aggravation, dreariness and lack of incentives or rewards.

Women resent their husband's demands for attention after having spent the day working, bracing against full and late busses, and standing in long lines in front of grocery stores, knowing that their efforts might be completely fruitless. Marital devotion takes second place when competing with expected, demanded and extracted revolutionary devotion.

Child care is also a source of frustration when control of the offspring is ultimately in the hands of the Revolution. One has to be concerned with the real fear of voicing, in front of one's children, comments and opinions that, if repeated, could be construed as antirevolutionary and involving dangerous consecuences. Besides, if one's children are to adapt to Castro's society, one cannot harm their future by fostering negative attitudes towards the Revolution.

Parents cannot control their children's behavior, because, once elementary school is finished, adolescents attend secondary schools which are scheduled in short shifts which result in their being left unattended and practically "in the streets" most of each day. Parental authority, challenged by revolutionary policy, has created a vacuum of authority where parents, at best, attempt to regulate the sexual behavior of the young girls, apparently with little success, especially when youngsters are sent to the country schools. Children soon learn that parental authority is limited, and, when too restrictive, can be successfully ignored and openly challenged with no great economic or social repercussions.

The Mariel interviewees commented that the youth, after *los viajes de la comunidad* (the Cuban exiled community visits), are very discontented and more verbally so than their elders. This perception appears to be supported by the youthfulness of the recent arrivals. They resent scarcity of consumer goods, the lack of control of their lives in matters of employment, housing, etc. They question the validity of a "free" educational system where there is no choice of careers. It is frustrating to live in a system where membership in revolutionary institutions weighs more than grades in the selective criteria for some of the careers, i.e., law, the humanities, etc. Many interviewees remarked with scorn about the official line that education in Cuba is free, since they feel that the forced "volunteer" work far outpays the cost of their educational fees and expenses. They greatly resent and resist forced indoctrination and military duty. Even though most of the youth are not too interested in political ideology, and politics is not openly discussed or much talked about, they resort to the traditional Cuban way of airing grievances by rejoicing in hearing and telling jokes at the expense of the government.

Cuban youth is outraged by their perceived disenfranchisement in their own homeland. They resent not being permitted access to certain neighborhoods, restaurants, stores, hotels and beaches in their own country, which are reserved for the "new class" and for foreigners. They are scornful of the display of affluence of the youth of the new class who drive Fiats and Ladas while wearing expensive Italian shoes and fashionable clothing. Their disadvantaged situation becomes more obvious when, by chance, they are exposed to places where the new class, in their view, enjoys "La Dolce Vita." Additionally, the youth greatly admire everything Western, especially American music, jeans and old American movies.

Long lasting romantic relationships are uncommon, due, perhaps, to the lack of trust and control in one's life. Romancing and infatuation are a means of escaping the dreary reality but hardly ever lead to a strong lasting commitment.

One thirty-two-year-old male reported that when he decided to enter the Peruvian Embassy, he failed to tell his wife because "he was afraid of how she was going to react if I told her about the plan." A twenty-year-old male informant commented, laughingly, "Romance, are you kidding? Romantic love belongs to history." A twenty-five-year-old female added, "Young people want to believe in love, to fantasize, but sex in Cuba is only an escape."

Housing shortages on the island limit the possibilities for privacy and intimacy. This, in many instances, prompts young lovers and even newlyweds, who live in crowded conditions, to patronize for a few hours at a time sleazy hotels set up by the government for such purposes. Lines in front of these hotels are very long, but the humiliating experience is endured despite the exposure to possibly indiscreet witnesses.

2. Religion. Participation in religious activities in Cuba has greatly decreased. This is due to the direct discouragement and indirect persecution by the government of those who frequent churches, since they are suspected of counterrevolutionary attitudes. Thus, former religious holidays such as Christmas, Good Friday, Easter, the Feast of the Epiphany, etc., which traditionally set the rhythm, of the former Cuban calendar, have been eliminated and replaced by revolutionary holidays. Revolutionary indoctrination emphasizes historical events which present a negative picture of religion such as the Inquisition, Galileo's Trial, religious wars, etc. Derisive comments about religious people are constantly made during doctrinal training.

The youth fear reprisals from the government if religious affiliation were to be known. Religious activity could be considered improper and suspicious behavior, which would mean the loss of opportunities to obtain scholarships or to be able to pursue some careers. Many of the younger informants identified themselves as atheists. Some reported having been baptised secretly. Most people are married in civil ceremonies for fear of government reprisal. Many churches have been closed and those which are not, normally open their side doors.

Apparently, the majority of church goers are senior citizens who have nothing to loose.

Informants say that the new Cuban Constitution reflects a more tolerant attitude toward formal religion. However, during the Mariel boatlift the Jehova's Witnesses, called "Los Patiblancos" (the white feet), who have been greatly persecuted in Cuba because of their resistance to integrating into the system, were forced out and given preferential treatment to abandon the island. It is apparent that the loyalty of the Cuban population to institutionalized religion is not very strong. During the early years of the Revolution, many of the victims of the *paredón* (execution wall), died exclaiming *"Viva Cristo Rey"* (long live Christ the King). However, in general, organized religion and especially the Catholic Church, which was the religion of preference, failed to be a rallying point for the people dissatisfied with materialistic communism. This might be due to the superficiality of the Catholic affiliation of the popular masses in Cuba. This situation contrasts with the important role that Catholicism has played in Poland, where it is a symbol of resistance to communism, despite the country's having common frontiers with Russia. It appears that Cubans' Catholic affiliation, as expressed by the pre-revolutionary idiomatic expression, *"Yo soy católico a mi manera"* (I am Catholic in my own way), reflected an accommodative lip-service position towards religion which lacked dogmatic loyalty and deep commitment. Otherwise, it is difficult to understand the sudden decline of religious fervor in favor of atheism, agnosticism, and affiliation with magical-religious complexes.

Many informants reported that non-Christian religious systems, such as Afrocuban *Santería* and Spiritism, have either maintained or expanded their following. This situation might be due to the fact that, even though, officially, the government scorns these cult organization practices, they are not perceived as dangerous to the regime, since they don't pose the threat that institutionalized religion does. Also, as in the case of *Santería* and other Afrocuban religious complexes, due to Cuba's political aspirations in Africa (36) and its pitch towards Black people and culture, the government sees fit to officially sponsor African-influenced art and literature, even those with religious themes.

It is interesting to note that *Santería* in the United States has also gained prestige, acceptability and following among Cuban exiles (37). *Santería* functions as a support system and mediating institution (38) for Miami Cubans suffering acculturative stress. It could be theorized that the prevailing conditions in Cuba which contribute to feelings of lack of control, ambivalence, stress, and loss, are even more conducive to enhancing a people's dependence upon magical systems as a means of obtaining supernatural support to deal with their lives.

3. The Mask. Prevalent conditions on the Island are the basis for the individual's need to constantly strive to act out a role that is incompatible with self identification and ego development. Informants normally refer to themselves as people wearing a mask; some of them, the older ones, in a conscious manner. Younger informants say that, without realizing it, they just learn the appropriate thing to say and do. According to a thirty five year old male informant, for example:

> We try to tell or look like something others will accept. We are incapable of doing things which are good for ourselves. The Revolution kills the capacity to create. I have conditioned myself by reflex to say whatever the other person wants to hear.

This is done by a process of auto-censorship (39). According to *Miami Herald* reporter, Liz Balmaseda, who visited friends and relatives in her native town, this programmed acting out and use of the mask is prevalent on the island. "They said all the right things and did what they were supposed to do." Balmaseda reports that there were cracks though, in the form of jokes and laughter. "Do you see this face? this is not my real face, only a mask. Here we live with masks; we have no other choice. We can't say anything against the government. We are scared to death of the government." Another friend of Balmaseda's added, "Of course we all live with masks." Yet one person involved in the conversation reacted angrily when under humorous threat to uncover his face and be left without the protective mask, "Shut up. If you are going to talk, why don't you go to the middle of the street and cry your heart out so everyone will hear you? Because you are a coward" (40).

The author once had a similar experience when she found herself in the middle of a conversation that turned into a confrontation between a son who had arrived from Mariel and his mother, who was visiting from Cuba. The mother told the son, "You just be careful, they will get you here and anywhere you hide. Do you think you are safe because you are in Miami?" Then, turning to the author, "God knows what might happen to you and your curiosity." The author interpreted the incident as a desperate protective reaction, i.e., "How do you, my own son, dare to face me with reality? How dare you pull my mask away? Don't you see that I cannot go back to Cuba without it?"

Thus, one needs to constantly concern oneself with avoiding any type of behavior which could be interpreted as antirevolutionary. This is so, because any act can be deemed or miscounstrued as "improper" (41) or "anti-revolutionary," which could lead to all types of margination, reprisal, incarceration and even death. In this regard a thirty-five-year-old male informant related the following:

> My parents were always angry with me, because I liked to sunbathe in the backyard. They claimed that members of the Committee for de Defense of the Revolution could label me as lazy and as lumpen (42). I argued that the Committee knew better than anybody else that I had a full time job and that I was also going to college. However, they convinced me that my demeanor, relaxed and non chalant, was defiance. I stopped sunbathing in my own backyard.

These masked people are always passive. In a passive way they don't air any opinions and passively participate in revolutionary life and repeat revolutionary slogans. The "true believers" try to convince them that participation in revolutionary activities is convenient and rewarding; they try to compromise others with the system. Thus, the masked segments of the population, according to informants, are the majority of the people who are hoarded into the Revolutionary Plaza, attend the meetings of the Committees for the Defense of the Revolution, while inwardly rejecting or enduring them.

According to a twenty-year-old female informant, "Everybody simulates; they appear to be what they are not; they act busy and don't accomplish anything." This constant autocensorship and wearing of a mask causes a state of constant anxiety, nervousness and depression, which is also the root of a basic paranoid personality suffering from insomnia and restlessness. The young psychiatrists who worked for the author confided, after some time, that the use of tranquilizers in Cuba is appalling and claimed that a few of their patients were afraid to go to sleep for fear of talking while asleep.

A large number of informants told the author that, in Cuba, people were overstimulated by perennial crisis, frustration, overcrowdness, lack of privacy, etc. A twenty-year old male informant said, "They force us to go to the fields, even though we accomplish nothing. Their goal is keeping us groggy, without time to reflect and think. *Cuba es una vorágine* (Cuba is a whirlpool)." This enforced activity and social participation cause hyperactivity which further strengthens anxiety and depression. Most of those interviewed demonstrated and reported the need in Cuba to be always with others in an effort to gain support, as much information as possible, and control.

A thirty-five-year-old male informant commented as follows:

Cubans on the island are more gregarious than the Cubans in Dade County. We are more sociable; we share more. At night I always had some visitors, or I went around the neighborhood, or to visit friends. Cuban Americans are *casa sola* (house loners), more selfish. They like to be by themselves. I asked him, "Do you go out or entertain visitors every night in Miami?" He was taken by surprise and answered: "No!" "Is it that you are more tired here than in Cuba?" "No!", he answered. "Why don't you go out here every night?" "I don't know." "Why did you always need to be with people in Cuba?" Well, they gave me support. I felt their company reassured me. I felt supported. Besides, you know everybody in the neighborhood; you always meet them at meetings, in the lines in front of the stores, everywhere. "Weren't you tired of visiting with them? Did you also visit people you didn't really like or trust?" Well, yes, but... "Did you feel you had to pretend to enjoy their company so as not to raise their possible enemity?" My goodness, that is true. Also, at lunch break I went to talk to my friends to see if they could assist me in solving some problem; maybe I needed some material or something for the house or anything.. Yes, it is all right to be by yourself in Miami, in Cuba it is not.

According to a thirty-one-year old informant:

"Life in Cuba requires one to be always on the look out and in a perennial state of alertness. One is always seeking opportunities to obtain what one needs while fearing to be caught in black market transactions. One is always afraid that a member of the Comité (Committee for the Defense of the Revolution) might search your bag and find some goods. One is afraid of being caught exchanging food for clothes with a farmer. One is afraid of being found out absent from a revolutionary meeting; one is afraid of doing anything."

In such an atmosphere of distrust, lack of control and ambivalence, rational thinking, planning and reasoning are useless. This frustrating environment prompts emotional reactions, anxiety, and regression to less mature non-rational states. Wishful thinking takes the place of planning and reasoning. According to an informant: "When I felt very frustrated and anxious I used to tell myself: 'I am going to leave Cuba.' I didn't do anything about it, but that simple wish calmed my anxiety."

When wishful thinking (the official line of propaganda) is privately practiced and verbally expressed amidst fear and doubt, it turns into rumor which, upon return to the individual, is eagerly believed and repeated again to others as a ray of hope or life raft. Over and over again the hopeful rumor goes: "Fidel has cancer" which projects the contained anger and aggression that cannot be expressed overtly. Wishful thinking, rumor, make believe; all of them contribute greatly to the need to avoid facing up to the gloomy reality of their hopeless lives.

Loyalty, commitment, and interdependency are dulled by distrust and paranoia which further erodes feelings of self integrity. Bourgeois morality, which shaped prerevolutionary conscience, has been shattered and replaced by meaningless revolutionary slogans quite alien to the individual's need for self assurance and attempts to satisfy basic drives. The prevalent and only theme of the Cuban ethos is to survive at any cost.

Joking and making fun of one's own misery, which are traditional Cuban ways of venting anger and relieving tension, are the healthier mechanisms of survival. Nevertheless, all of these strategies are attempts to avoid total submission and achieve some degree of control. Thus, the Cubans on the island are legitimate heroes in their own right. Those failing to accept a system of terror, oppression and ambiguity have utilized whatever coping mechanisms allowed them to resist the system and survive.

V

THE MARIELITOS AND
NATIONAL IDENTITY

The "Marielitos" as a Cuban population group have already been described in terms of the life they endured in Cuba and the reasons that propelled them from Mariel to Miami. They must also be viewed as a group that represents aspects of the Cuban personality as it underwent the transformation caused by Castro and his revolution.

The French nineteenth century writer, Ernest Renan, said that a nation is a soul made up by the possession of a rich legacy of memories and the will to preserve the (undivided) inheritance that has been passed down to it. A nation is having the common glories of the past, a common will to do in the present, having done the great things of the past, and wishing to do more of the same in the future.

A. Cuban Historical Experience

The Republic of Cuba was less than fifty-seven years old when Castro's Revolution triumphed. History recounts Cuban colonial experience (1512-1898) as a period of interaction and merging of the regionally diverse Spanish culture of the colonists with the few Amerindian traits which survived colonization and the strong input of different African cultures brought by the slaves.

On the other hand, Cuban's insularity and geographic position dominating the Caribbean, turned the island into a natural bridge between the northern and the southern hemispheres of the New World and also between Hispanic America and Spain (44). During most of the colonial period the harbor of Havana was the meeting place for the Spanish fleet which, loaded with treasures, merchandise, travelers and visitors, sailed to and from the metropolis. This geographic factor had great political, economic and social repercussion due to the convergence in the island of still other cultural influences of Caribbean, Central, South and North American, as well as French and English extraction. This constant cultural contact greatly influenced the way of life and worldview of its inhabitants.

Spanish culture was, by far, the most influential in shaping Cuban culture, imprinting it with values shared by other Hispanic nations such as the strong family orientation, personalism, individualism, *caudillismo* (Loyalty to a strong leader), a humanist orientation in education, etc. Cuba was one of the Hispanic American nations which most relished its Hispanic heritage and felt especially close to the Mother Country and its cultural traditions (45). This might be due to the fact that Cuba and Puerto Rico remained as colonies of Spain until 1898, long after the other American colonies had severed their ties in the first quarter of the nineteenth century. The prolonged colonial status turned the island into a favored place of settlement for Spaniards during the last century. This process continued during Republican times (1902-1851), demonstrating the lack of ill feeling between Cubans and Spaniards even though the former had fought for over thirty years to gain independence from the latter.

The Spanish colonial experience did not prepare the island for self rule. The Spanish government was authoritarian and centralized, leaving no room for democratic processes or self determination, since local governments had little or no power. The official Catholic Church had further stressed authoritarianism, centralization and the monarchical hierarchical organization. During three centuries Spain imposed merchantilistic economic policies, thereby limiting the possibilities for the economic development of the island. The government controlled commerce, industry and agriculture and imposed monopolistic policies whenever convenient to protect the economic interests of Spain. The colony languished, poor and underdeveloped.

In the 18th century some important educational, social and economic events occurred. In 1728 the Royal and Pontifical University of San Gerónimo was founded in Havana. The curriculum stressed the study of Thomistic philosophy and rhetoric emphasizing a humanistic and theological approach to knowledge. In 1762 Havana was conquered by the English who, during the year of occupation, opened the harbor to free commerce which led to some economic development. In 1781 the Seminario San Carlos was founded, and the principles of empirical science, emphasizing observation and experimentation, were taught in the island.

Also, at the end of the 18th century there was a movement led by Spanish governors and Cuban intellectuals which was geared to improving the economic, social, educational and sanitary conditions of the Island. Cuba began to have an interest in sugar production (46). This trend was further strengthened when the French colony of Haiti became independent, and the sugar economy of that island collapsed.

French refugees from Haiti settled in Cuba, bringing the knowledge to cultivate coffee and, also, helping Cuba develop into the sugar bowl of the world. The increase in sugar production created a great demand for African slaves, who were imported in impressive numbers to man the plantations.

At the beginning of the nineteenth century, when most of the colonies of Spain achieved independence, the Spanish government liberalized its policies in Cuba. The ensuing free trade brought significant economic resurgence. The island donned a new physiognomy. Monumental architecture sprang up, interest in educaton increased, and a refined way of life was adopted by the rich, among them an emerging Cuban Creole class of sugar plantation owners (47). However, Cuba remained backwards, a predominantly slave society, suffering from underdevelopment of its natural and human resources and from political authoritarianism and depotism, as well as great social injustices and inequalities.

During the nineteenth century, a definite Cuban mentality and character began to emerge (48). Teachers, poets and writers spoke of and taught about a distinctive national identity different from that of the Spaniards. The Romantic movement in literature echoed these nationalistic feelings and sang to the beauty of the country and of its yearnings for independence and freedom. Cuba's benign climate, the intimate scale of its rivers, mountains, valleys and savannahs inspired in its poets, composers and inhabitants feelings of closeness and harmony which constituted the core of a national identity. Later, Cubans perceived the island in an animistic fashion as a melancholic, sensual young woman with whom they related in intimate, personalistic terms. Cuba, tall, graceful, and brunette, was a good and nourishing mother...

Cuba's nationalistic yearnings spurred two wars of independence against Spanish rule. The first war (1868-1878) was primarily led by the well-to-do Creole class. It was inspired by romantic ideals influenced by the teachings of the French revolutionaries and philosophers who espoused individualism, freedom and equality. Many leaders of the nationalistic revolution however, came from the most humble classes with significant participation of free blacks who joined in the struggle and gained the admiration of all. Among them, Antonio Maceo became one of the most revered Cuban heroes. Black slaves, freed by their freedom-fighter Creole owners and encouraged by them to join the Cuban armies, played an important role. The first war of independence raged for ten years, causing the economic ruin of many of the Creole landowners who had led the independentist struggle. After Spain's victory and the peace settlement (1878), many Cubans went to live in the United States and other neighboring nations as exiles.

In 1895 the second war of independence started, inspired by the leadership of José Martí, a writer and a poet. Martí was an idealist who preached the active participation of all Cubans in the democratic Republic he dreamed of. His revolutionary ideology was based in racial equality, human dignity and a sense of brotherhood that included all Cubans and Spaniards who wished to participate.

In 1898, the United States government, which had become increasingly interested in Cuba because of growing commercial ties and imperialistic ambitions, intervenes in the island (49). Many American presidents and leaders had expressed geopolitical reasons why Cuba should be part of the sphere of influence of their nation. Several attempts had been made to purchase the island. Cuban exiles in the States had often experienced disappointment and bitterness caused by the ambivalent posture of the federal government, which in some instances, encouraged the patriots while also undermining their efforts. In the 1890's several armed expeditions were prepared in South Florida to help Cuban patriots on the island; yet, at the last minute the United States government seized the boats. Martí, who founded his revolutionary party among Cuban exiles in the States, often expressed great concern about what he feared would be the consequences of the unbridled ambitions of pro-imperialistic factions in American society if they were ever unleashed in the island.

In 1898, while war ravaged the island and decimated the population, the American Congress, prompted by the explosion of an American warship in Havana harbor, passed a Joint Resolution, declaring that Cuba had the right to be free. The United States government declared war against Spain. American forces destroyed the Spanish Fleet in Santiago harbor and, with the assistance of Cuban revolutionary armies, defeated the Spaniards in Oriente. These events marshalled extensive intervention in the island.

After more than thirty years of war, Cuba's economy was practically destroyed; health conditions were abominable; illiteracy was staggering; the remnants of the public administration system were disorganized; and people were confused by the unexpected ending of the war epic. American intervention lasted four years. During this time the military leaders in command implemented policies to create a new public administration system with emphasis placed upon sanitary policies and education. The United States government requested the election of delegates for a Cuban Constitutional Assembly. This assembly wrote a constitution for the new nation but was forced to accept the Platt Ammendment, a constitutional curtailment of Cuba's sovereignty. Later, elections were held and the first president was inaugurated on May 20th, 1902.

An aftermath of the United States intervention and the Platt Ammendment (50) was the decisive influence that it began to exercise in the young republic. U.S.A. companies purchased large tracks of land from its impoverished owners (51), while other firms invested in railroads, electric plants and other essential utilities and industries. Thus, Cuba's economy became vulnerable to the abuses of power of these companies (52). In many instances they influenced the federal government to coerce the Cuban government into accepting treaties and policies which were detrimental to Cuban national interests. During the 1930's the Platt Ammendment was abolished, and a proccess began that culminated in the purchase of considerable tracks of Cuban land by Cubans. American interference in Cuba's affairs, whether overt or covert, contributed to a Cuban mentality labeled "Plattista," an attitude of fatalistic and guarded acceptance of American interference. Interventions, even though resented, were also expected and, in some instances (Bay of Pigs), desired.

Cuba was not well-equipped economically, socially or politically to deal with the task of determining its own destiny when it emerged as an independent nation. The heavy-handed influence of the U.S. further hindered the efforts of the young republic to deal with the task successfully .

Political inestability permeated the republican experience. Authoritarian rulers, nepotism, corruption, and coup d'etats prompted civil disturbances and revolutionary strife (53). All of this created a climate of insecurity, distrust and antagonism toward political processes. Economic dependence on sugar caused instability and cyclical unemployment and underemployment patterns.

The republic had gone a long way to achieve racial integration. Even though Cubans of Spanish descent played a predominant role in the history of the island, blacks and mullatoes also contributed greatly to Cuban culture and worldview. Cuban society was more open to blacks than other societies, such as the United States (54).

Interethnic relations developed in a more cohesive and harmonious way. This was due to specific historical reasons. Spanish law forbade the sale of a slave without his nuclear family and allowed greater opportunities for the slave to make money and purchase his freedom. Since most Spanish settlers avoided engaging in occupations requiring manual skills, urban slaves had opportunities to become craftmen and gain some income. Also, during colonial times a mixture of population occurred when Spanish and Creole males had children with black concubines. Many of these white fathers cared for and supported their children. Such factors were responsible for the growth of a lower middle class of black and mulatto freemen long before Cuba gained independence from Spain.

In Cuba, blackness was a relative concept, not an absolute one as it is in the United States. Thus, the closer an individual was to the white population in physical appearance and social behavior, the greater the chances for social and economic mobility. During pre-revolutionary times intermarriage between whites of the lower classes with mulattoes and blacks, even though frowned upon, was fairly common.

Public school integration was mandated at the beginning of the Republic despite U.S. pressure to the contrary. There was residential integration, except for the very exclusive suburban neighborhoods in Havana. Blacks, however, had not yet achieved equal access to resources. A mitigating factor was that it was not until the 1940's that a significant growth of the middle class occurred. Even then, under and unemployment prevailed disregarding racial lines.

Blacks greatly contributed to all aspects of Cuban culture, especially music, poetry, the theater and athletics. International recognition was gained by Cuban rhythms highly influenced by African music, such as congas, guarachas, etc

In spite of many problems, important social and economic gains were achieved during the first fifty years of independence (55). Cuba developed one of the largest, most skilled middle class whose members enjoyed one of the highest standards of living in Hispanic America. The advanced social and labor legislation, as well as the aggressive negotiations of trade unions, resulted in the development of a strong and vocal working class with retirement, medical and maternity benefits. Professional and white collar workers created organizations to lobby for their special interests. A vast network of primary prevention clinics and, also, hospitals, was developed with government funding. In addition, a large number of privately run clinics offered, at minimum cost, preventive outpatient an hospitalization services to the urban populations. Public education had been instrumental in lowering the illiteracy rate from 45% for males and 55% for females in 1899 to 24% and 20% respectively in 1953 (56).

In the 1950's an admosphere of progress, expanded civil liberties and economic growth became evident. This was in part due to the confidence generated by a short period of political stability, and to the emergence, of small industries as result of the economic incentive granted by the government to Cuban nationals. Important also was the acquisition and increasing control by Cubans of agricultural lands formerly owned by foreign interests. The spectacular rise of tourism and the beginning of successful agricultural diversification also contributed greatly to economic development. However, multiple problems still plagued the young republic; among them, dependency on sugar, partial control of the economy by American and foreign companies, high unemployment and underemployment, a still high rate of illiteracy, political immaturity, and the need for social reforms responsive to the plight of landless peasants. Thus, the essential conditions necessary to develop a robust core of national identity were there, despite the failures to incorporate the totality of the population (especially peasants) into the enjoyment of the resources and into the sharing of the national experience and the forging of a common future. A large segment of the island's population, which included mostly blacks, unskilled workers and a majority of peasants, were neither the beneficiaries nor the actors in the important strides of the nation. Much was left to be achieved. Batista's coup d'etat in 1952 interrupted institutional life, and both repressive and revolutionary activities followed. This opened the way for Castro's revolution and its eventual success in 1959.

At this juncture, Cantro's revolution triumphed. Castro's movement had been primarily nourished and supported by members of the middle class who were searching for a definition of national identity and destiny (57). Castro, deceptively called the revolution, "As Cuban as the royal palm trees," and promised to restore democratic processes and to bring about social justice by an inclusive and concerted effort of all Cubans to forge a common future. However, contrary to Castro's early claims, the revolution never intended to restore democratic processes or civil liberties. It failed, also, to integrate all Cubans around a national identity new or otherwise (as manifested by the massive exodus).

This paper will analyze some of the most important factors which contribute to the formation of a national identity in order to determine whether or not Castro's regime, indeed, has been able to integrate Cuban society around an ethos. These factors are the following: (1) cultural continuity, evolution and syncretism; (2) cultural congruence and integration around value orientations; and (3) national character.

B. Formative Factors of National Identity

1. Cultural Continuity, Evolution and Syncretism. The twenty-five-year revolutionary experience represents a drastic, premeditated breakdown of what had been the process of formation of Cuba's national identity. There have been radical changes in the political, economic and social structures, but also a de facto repudiation of things Cuban. The Revolution apparently did not find anything worth keeping, except to continue the former Republic's strides to make education and health services available to greater segments of the population, while claiming exclusive credit for such advances.

Cuba's history has been revised and rewritten according to revolutionary dogma. Former heroes have been discredited and substituted by foreign ones (Marx, Lenin, etc.). Former traditions, e.g., Easter, Christmas, etc., have been repudiated as oppressive and reactionary symbols, while new festivities, all of them imbued with revolutionary ideology, have been imposed. Former emotional and cultural ties with Hispanic nations have been neglected or repudiated, in favor of solidarity with socialist and Third World nations, whose experiences áre alien to Cubans and their idiosyncrasies. Massive propaganda geared to cement these new allegiances and idols have, to all intents and purposes, created a nation of amnesiacs capable only of repeating *ad infinitum* the new revolutionary slogans, which, when challenged, are easily discarded and abandoned. Former friends have turned into enemies and former enemies are reputedly friends. Cuba is a country without memories.

According to a thirty-two-year-old male informant:

"Cuba is a clean slate, but the erasures erased our souls, our lives, our security, our objectives, our very essence and reason to live. We have been told, 'You are absolutely wrong. You are worthless, everything has to be changed. The Revolution is the teacher who is going to instruct you on how to think, reason and feel. You have to do and say whatever we tell you. You are incapable of thinking and acting by yourselves.' They have changed the names of provinces, streets, schools, everything. Sometimes I have wondered if it was all a nightmare intended to make us all go crazy. Some of us did go crazy, and for what? Nobody feels comfortable or at home because it is no longer our island; it is the island of the Revolution and of those few who are the Revolution."

Cuba's former nourishing institutions, family, friends, religion, have been shattered by the overwhelming intolerance and demands of revolutionary ideology.

Cubans' personalistic image of the island, as a giving nourishing mother in intimate relationships with her children, has been destroyed. According to a thirty-six-year-old male informant of peasant background:

"When I was ten years old I visited Viñales and in that place I experienced great intimacy with Cuba, with its palm trees, its transparent air, its soft breeze. Two years before I came, I went back to Viñales, but it was empty; it had no soul."

Another informant, a thirty-eight year old male tells about a trip to Santiago and how, from the plane, he watched a great number of palm trees being bulldozed to make room for some experimental agricultural project. Sadly he said to himself, "There is nothing left of Cuba. Cuba now is nothing but a materialistic geographic reality. Cuba is no longer the sweet home of my ancestors. Cuba is no longer nourishing; she doesn't manifest herself anymore as she is.

The romantic, quasi-mystical perception of Cuba has been lost. One young informant, a student at Miami-Dade Community College, commented sadly, "Cuba is a prison." Another replied in response to a question, "Are you kidding? Are you asking me if the youth feel an intimate attachment to the island? I will tell you. No. Cubans see Cuba as another world in which you are locked in and cannot get out. I don't ever want to go back."

A twenty-year-old female informant remarked that, "People in Miami adore Cuba; they have a passion for it. Cubans in Cuba don't feel sorry for her, they don't love her."

On the basis of such information one may surmise that Cuba is undergoing a process of deculturation whereby most former institutions and traditions have not been allowed to survive, evolve or syncretize with the new ways of the Revolution. This situation is a source of great alienation in the majority of the population. It inhibits an integration around a national ethos or identity.

2. Cultural Congruence and Integration Around Value Orientation. Since there has been an overt effort to curtail cultural continuity and evolution by forceful discontinuation of old cultural traditions, open discouragement of others and the imposition of alien ones, a question arises concerning the extent to which this process has been successful. Notwithstanding the forced acquiescence to the regime's mandate by participation in "free elections," mass rallies and the like, it is incumbent upon us to assess the extent to which an intrinsic internalization of the new communist culture and worldview "a la Castro" has occurred. Also, it is important to assess the degree of consonance between the avowed ideal, the officially sponsored behavioral patterning, and those patterns exhibited and developed by the people in order to survive. Since values give a culture a sense of direction, of "oughtness," delineating behavioral models and ideals; it is worthwhile to compare the value orientation of Castro's regime with that of the people.

Florence Kluckhohn developed a theory of value orientations and their influence upon normative behavior. To Kluckhohn, "Value orientations are complex but definitely patterned (rank ordered) principles, resulting from the transactional interplay of three analytically distinguishable elements of the evaluative process -the cognitive, the affective, and the directive elements- which give order and direction to the ever-flowing stream of human acts and thoughts as these relate to the solution of 'common human' problems" (58). Values are important factors affecting a society's worldview, existential philosophy and meaning, life expectations, etc..

According to Kluckhohn, there are some universal problems which confront all societies and people, which can be solved by a limited range of variations. A society might be characterized by the preference for a given solution to a specific problem —dominant value oriention— but variant solutions or values are also present and essential to well being.

Kluckhohn identified five universal problems which every society has to confront and for which it must provide solutions. These problems are the following: (a) the temporal focus of human life, (b) the relation of man to nature and supernature, (c) the form of man's relation to other men, (d) the modality of human activity, and (e) the character of innate human nature. Kluckhohn's five universal problems allow the possibilities of three different solutions to each of them.

Using Kluckhohn's theoretical framework, Dr. Hazel Weidman and collaborators conducted comparative research on value orientations and health beliefs and practices of Black Americans, Bahamians, Cubans, Haitians and Puerto Ricans residing in Dade County (59). This research yielded significant data concerning the syncretic nature of the value orientation of the Cuban population, since none of the preferred solutions showed significantly in comparison to the other variant solutions. These results, apparently, are characteristic of cultures in transition. They are found in societies which are in a process of accommodation to a dominant culture. During the process of assimilation some features from the dominant culture are borrowed, while traditional values are preserved. This results in a cultural syncretism, the process which has been taking place on the island of Cuba for five hundred years.

No value orientation study was ever carried out in pre-revolutionary Cuba. Reflections upon this subject and the apparent syncretic nature of pre-revolutionary Cuba's value orientation have been discussed elsewhere by the author (60). Studies done with some Hispanic Latin American groups show clear-cut directions with respect to value orientation. However, the Cuban experience, always rich with cultural contacts and borrowings shows an eclectic, opportunistic accommodation and points to the syncretic nature of the Cuban culture in a fashion suggested by the Miami Health Ecology Project research findings (61).

If the process of cultural syncretism, which has been such an integral part of the Cuban experience during the last five hundred years were still occurring in the island today, revolutionary dogma would have been at least partially internalized by the mayority of the population. Thus, a value orientation research would yield a slanted preference towards the solutions sponsored by the government. The second order of preference would probably reflect the solutions preferred in pre-revolutionary times. Such preferences made a strong showing in the Cuban American sample of the Miami Health Ecology Project research and are shared by many Latin societies.

However, there is, apparently, an unresolved clash between the official communist system value orientation and the one manifested by the majority of Mariel refugees. Presumably this conflict is also prevalent in large segments of Cubans on the island.

Regarding the Time orientation or the temporal focus of human life, each society appraises the importance of behavior in terms of either maintaining Past traditions, considering Future repercussions, or resolving Present problems. Latin societies, characteristically, have shown a pronounced preference for a Present Time orientation, which the author assumes was, also, the preference in pre-revolutionary Cuba. The Miami research findings show Present Time orientation as a weak preference over Past Time orientation among Dade County Cubans; while Past is weakly preferred over the Future (62).

In Cuba, the official preferred Time orientation (which is also prevalent in American culture) is that of the Future. Communist systems, with their planned economies, are always geared toward the Future. However, Cubans, despite constant slogans and massive revolutionary propaganda, have not internalized a Future Time orientation. This might be due to the failure of most plans and, also, that the only ones who plan are the planners themselves, who show little sympathy for the opinions of those for whom they plan. In exchange, the executioners of the plan, those who are acted upon, demonstrate great feelings of lack of control, conscious or unconscious distrust of the plans, and a strong Present Time orientation, possibly stronger than it was before the Revolution. Immediate gratification, with no questions about its consequences, appears to be functional in a society where one does't know what tomorrow will bring. According to one informant, "You buy with your money whatever you can get; otherwise you might lose your chance to buy anything." It is interesting to notice that among Cuban Americans the shock of acculturation has resulted in the syncretism of the dominant U.S. value orientation and that of their own culture in a very eclectic way.

The Man-Nature orientation deals with a society's perception of its relationship with the environment, nature and supernatural. When the people feel Subjugated to Nature, humans perceive themselves as helpless when confronting natural and supernatural forces, a situation which is accepted in fatalistic fashion. In other societies, humans perceive nature as being ordered by laws and principles, which, when known by science, may be harnessed by technology and placed at the service of human beings. Humans see themselves as Mastering or Controlling their relationships with nature. Yet, in other societies, humans see themselves as inseparable from nature and in Harmonious relationship with it. Hispanic societies, in general, have shown a preference towards the Subjugation orientation, which the author believes was also preferred by a majority of Cubans in pre-revolutionary times. On the other hand, as already pointed out, deep feelings of Harmony were also present with respect to the specific physical experience of the island. The Miami-based research showed a weak preference of Mastery over Subjugation, with the latter also making a weak showing over Harmony. Mastery Over Nature is the preferred value orientation of American and communist societies. The Miami findings (63) show the effect that acculturation is having on the worldview of Cuban Americans who are borrowing, in an eclectic fashion, some of the values of the dominant society. In contrast, the Mariel informants demonstrate a definite Subjugation orientation contrary to the communist regime. As already indicated, this has been the traditional orientation in Hispanic societies. It has always entailed, however, the existence of an overwhelming mystical supernatural power and the fatalistic acceptance of destiny driven by such forces. The loss of the monotheistic belief in an overpowering, orderly, fair supernatural force has produced insurmountable feelings of hopelessness and merciless suffering with no redemptive features. The chaotic Cuban experience, the uncertainty and unpredictability of the situation has given greater credibility to those religious beliefs, such as Santería, which render cult to amoral, capricious and unpredictable super natural forces and utilize magical means to control them. As Mariel informants often verbalized it, *"La Revolución es mucho para un solo corazón"* (The Revolution is too much for just one heart) or, *"Me da lo mismo por Zapata que por la Doce"* (It is the same to get there by Zapata or Twelve Street) referring to the streets that converge at the entrance to the Havana cemetery.

A twenty-eight-year old female student and factory worker stated that "People are rebellious and frustrated with all aspects of life, because one is impotent with the Revolution " Adding, "Everything is the same, a frustration; one has to *aturdirse* (purposefully confuse one's self) to be able to cope."

The Relational orientation deals with the nature of a person's relations to other people. If the society has a Lineal orientation, authority which is highly valued, revolves arround a vertical hierarchical scheme. When a society has a Collateral orientation, people relate to others acording to a horizontal network and on the basis of equality and interdependency. The Individualistic orientation leads people to relate to others according to their own perceptions and interests in an autonomous fashion with little consideration for vertical or lateral frames.

Individualism, Spanish style, entails a different set of directions and perceptions than American individualism does. Individualism among Hispanics is an assertion of Being, of self-worth, of uniqueness in no way narrowed by restrictive self-interest. Individualism, American style, is more geared to the achievement of economic independence or self determination. In most Hispanic societies the Lineal orientation is prevalent. The author believes that in pre-revolutionary Cuba, despite the strong presence of the Spanish brand of Individualism, the Lineal and the Collateral preferences were stronger.

The Miami Health Ecology Project findings from the Cuban sample (64) show Individualism as a weak preference over Collateral which is weakly preferred over Lineal. Again, the Individualistic orientation, so strongly preferred in American culture, is having an impact upon Cuban American society. It is a strategy which, in their context, enhances control over their lives.

The official orientation of Castro's Cuba is Lineal, emphasizing Castro as the Supreme Authority and embodiment of the Revolution and the one and only decision maker. Unbounded, unlimited and unquestionable loyalty is owed to him, his revolution and the party-line. However, among those Mariel entrants interviewed, despite their admitted submission to totalitarian authority, there were obvious demonstrations of resentment and defiance of authority which they viewed as abusive, oppressive and non-rewarding. This attitude toward authority spills over into other areas outside of politics, including parents, the elderly, teachers and all the former symbols of authority, experience and wisdom. Resistance, Cuban style, has been manifested in poor or non-collaboration with the authoritarian system. This is prompted by either mere frustration or conscious desire to sabotage the old Hispanic axiom, *"Obedezco pero no cumplo"* (I obey but don't accomplish). Self-serving Individualism is the preferred orientation in Cuba; however, it merely facilitates naked survival as reflected in the expression, *"Sálvese quien pueda"*

(Everyone for himself).

Interestingly, among those interviewed, the Collateral orientation is still strong despite the prevalence of distrust and paranoia expressed by many informants who said, "If you get in trouble, nobody is going to help you; *cualquiera te echa palante* (anyone will expose you)." The individual stills seeks the company of others to gain some feelings of support even from people he doesn't necessarily trusts. However, a Collateral orientation, which encourages interdependency, is not the most viable preference in a society where distrust has survival value. Among Cuban Americans, on the contrary, Collateralism has been the basis for economic, social and political network, and has greatly enhanced the Cuban American adaptive process.

The Activity orientation deals with the way a society perceives and evaluates people's behavior according to the manner in which it is manifested. The Doing orientation implies that society values the use of time engaged in activities with measurable outcomes. On the other hand, those societies which are Being oriented, highly value activities which are manifestations of an individual's existential yearnings and expressions. Hispanic societies have traditionally shown a preference toward the Being orientation which, in a way, is but a reflection of Hispanic style individualism: "I am the way I am; I do whatever I feel like; I am the King in my house; I am who I am, and I am not going to change."

The author believes that Being was the prevalent orientation in pre-revolutionary Cuba where people would comment: *"Hay que trabajar para poder vivir"* (One has to work in order to be able to live), contrary to living for one's work. The Miami Health Ecology Project sample (65) shows a weak preference for Doing over Being, due to the Cuban American adoption of the value oriention of the dominant American culture. In contrast, communist ideology is dramatically opposed to individualistic Being and demands a strong Doing orientation: Volunteerism, revolutionary meetings, long work schedules, etc. The Mariel interviewees defy both choices, they are neither Doing oriented (which brings no material or moral reward) nor Being oriented with introspective and soul searching features which communism would perceive as selfish, narcissistic, possibly dissident and antirrevolutionary behavior. People in Cuba, more than being Being or Doing oriented, are escapists. According to a twenty-six-year old female informant, "People in Cuba spend their lives *masajeando* (dragging their feet). It is shameless. You don't get any rewards for your efforts, so you do the least. However, over there we are always tired because of the constant hassles, lines, long waits, etc. Life is hard, and one is involved in constant activity and hussling which, at the end, yield nothing."

The Human Nature orientation deals with society's perceptions of innate human qualities in terms of essential goodness or evilness. Societies which define human beings as innately Good have an optimistic view of human nature, perceiving man as good and rational but susceptible to being corrupted. Those societies which prefer the Evil orientation perceive man as basically evil but perfectible. If the society's orientation is neutral, man is perceived as neither Good nor Evil but quite susceptible to both good and evil circumstatial influences. Hispanic and Catholic Mediterranean societies, in general, have had the neutral orientation. The author believes that this orientation was preffered in pre-revolutionary Cuba.

In Castro's Cuba the official line is based upon an unrealistic dichotomy between the Supergoods and the Superevils. Revolutionaries and communists are good, pure, selfless and self-effacing; while counter revolutionaries and capitalists are selfish and destructive agents of evil. Those Mariel entrants interviewed did not perceive Human Nature as dichotomized symbols of the Marxist dialectic class struggle, but as both Good and Evil with the primacy of the evil elements. Man is seen as having no principles. The world is perceived as Evil and so are men, but they are excusable because of life circumstances. "They find excuses to justify everything," said the informants. The author believes that in the past the good elements outnumbered the negative ones. The change in respect to this perception might be due to the fact that, in Cuba, practically everyone has being forced to engage in some type of antisocial behavior. "Everybody steals in Cuba. To steal is part of surviving. The butcher steals meat; the storekeeper steals materials, etc. It is like a conspiracy Everybody covers for everybody else. You can steal all you can from the government, which will be perceived as the right thing to do, because the government is the greatest thief of them all."

On the other hand, the communist system labels as antisocial or inappropriate behavior (which could lead to punishment and ostracism) all types of activities. These include attempts to leave the island, openly professing a religious faith, being uncooperative with the government, etc., -activities which are not necessarily perceived by the people as being wrong. This generates paranoid feelings toward the world and even greater reliance on Cuban traditional empathic compassion to justify error. The system, which rigidly punishes and repudiates any behavior it considers inappropriate, is the same system which has encouraged a plundering mentality through the sacking of the possessions left behind by more than a million people who left the island. It is a system which cannot fail to elicit from those who endure it, very negative perceptions about the world as well as anti-social attitudes dictated by their need to survive. They are motivated to beat a system which forces them to steal, encourages them to expose others, and commit all types of aggression against those who have fallen in disgrace. It is not surprising that the view of human nature in Cuba is growing darker and darker.

The great disparity that exists between the Castro government's preferred value orientation and that of the people, suggests that the communist ideology which has been imposed on the Cuban people is only endured and not internalized. Communism's rejection of some Cuban traditions and values, has hindered the process of syncretism which might have ensured compliance and cultural consonance.

3. National Character

a) Pre-Castro national character traits. During the Cuban historical process, some salient characteristics of the Cuban character became identifiable, even though all of them were not universally shared by all segments of the population. In general, Cubans, like most Hispanics, were oriented to primary institutions as a source of security, support and loyalty. The bilaterally-extended family was the most important institution, and it permeated the life of each individual. The concept of family in Cuba included all relatives, in-laws, friends and even neighbors. Linguistically, this was reflected in the use of the term *familia* (family) when greeting and referring to people liked and loved and to whom privileges and obligations of kinsmen were extended. The strong family orientation was linked to the great importance given to friendship. Cubans were taught to "cultivate" friends. *Ser amigo de sus amigos* (Being a good friend) was considered a sign of wholeness, trustworthiness, selflessness. This orientation turned the ideal Cuban into a sharer of resources and love. In some instances, and understandably so, it justified nepotism. Family treatment was also extended to neighbors, following the old Spanish axiom, *¿Quién es tu hermano? Tu vecino más cercano* (Who is your brother? Your next door neighbor).

Personalism, the need to relate in personal terms and to avoid impersonal relations and situations, was related to the family orientation. Personalism emphasized trust in people known and distrust of institutions and laws which were too abstract and impersonal. Cubans, like most Hispanics, were taught to be very sociable and "open" -sharing with people they knew, information about their personal lives, aspirations, etc. In this type of culture, people were judged according to their behavior with family and friends and not by their public lives or performance in business. *El que no quiere a su madre no quiere a nadie* (He who doesn't love his mother or family doesn't love anybody) and *Ese no es amigo de nadie* (He is nobody's friend) were expressions used with individuals who were disliked, not-trusted and rejected, even if successful. Loyalty to personal relationships was demanded, even when reflected in behavior which did not benefit the community or the individual himself. *Ser fiel hasta la muerte* (Being loyal until death) was admired.

In such a culture life is seen as an interaction with other people. To enjoy life, others also have to enjoy it. Otherwise there is an imbalance. Things are not quite right. Misfortune will befall those who are self-serving. Thus, generosity was greatly admired, even when excessively shown. People spoke with admiration of overgenerous individuals who gave parties and would *tirar la casa por la ventana* (throw the house out the window). Many claimed *El dinero se hizo redondo para rodar* (Coins are round so they can roll) or *Tengo hoyos en los bolsillos* (I have holes in my pockets) or *El dinero me pica en las manos* (Money bites the hand) to express their perception that money was to be used, not accumulated. Thus, a person who was a *botarate* (threw his money) was liked if he used it with family and friends. Those who used it on themselves were seen as selfish and cheap.

Cubans admired people who showed empathy and compassion for others. Ever subjective, emotional and sentimental, Cubans always had excuses for people in difficult situations or those experiencing bad luck. This had to do with their perception of the frailty of human nature, and a consciousness of human vulnerability and mortality. Cubans, thus, tended to be lenient when judging themselves and others, always looking for extenuating circumstances to justify human flaws. *Me da pena con* (I fell sorry for) so and so, because he doesn't have a job, or is an alcoholic, or is ill-tempered, and he cannot help it. *Fulano es un buenazo, un infeliz* (So and so is good-natured, incapable of hurting a fly) and thus I empathize with him even though he doesn't do anything right. This orientation is reflected in the national pastime of *tirar toalla* (Throwing the towel) to those appearing to be at the end of their rope. These features reflect a very flexible, non-rigid attitude toward a both good and bad human nature, conflictful but in equilibrium. Linguistically, this is expressed by adding the diminutive *ito* (small) to nouns and names of people of whom we feel protective, such as children; e.g., Juanito or ethnic groups; e.g., *negrito, chinito* or a particular category of persons, e.g., *Marielitos*.

In summary, in order to be respected and admired, Cubans were expected to be friendly, generous, extroverted, and fun-loving. In other words, they had to be *campechanos* (no translation, but suggesting people who are generous, non-threatening, caring, trustworthy, and extremely engaging) or *buena gente* (good people) even when others might take advantage of their generosity and openness.

Cubans had a quasi-mystical attitude toward life. There was a fatalistic, acceptance of the view that men were subjugated to supernatural forces. Even though organized religion did not thoroughly channel this national trait, Cubans were concerned about their own mortality, the afterlife and the interaction between life and mystical forces. This cultural attitude is responsible for the growth of syncretic Afrocuban religious complexes and the experimentation with religious systems other than Catholicism. Cubans believe in luck as a factor affecting human life. Success was attributed to luck more than to diligence, which of course, made failure more tolerable than in societies when control over nature is assumed. *El pobre fulano no tiene suerte* (Poor soul, he is not lucky), which expressed empathy for a person without a job, skills, etc. The prevalent belief in *Mal de ojo* (evil eye) was part of the Cuban experience, and it gave rise to ambiguous expressions such as *No creo en la brujería, pero la respeto* (I don't believe in sorcery, but I respect it).

Another aspect of the ideal national character was to have a good sense of humor, to engage in and appreciate the exchange of jokes. Humor was expressed in two distinctive ways: *choteo* which was an individual's way of channeling aggression in a socially acceptable manner, and *relajo* which was a collective, defensive means of expressing frustration and releasing pain by using the art of laughter even at one's own expense.

Closely related to these traits was the quality of being *simpático*. This term does not involve being sympathetic but being witty, fun, and *tener tabla* (to have stage skills). The phrase, *en Cuba se puede ser todo menos pesao* (in Cuba any character flaw is tolerated if one is witty), was commonly used to express admiration for the over-sociable, overwitty personality to the extent that any detracting antisocial trait was disregarded.

Cuban personality was also characterized by a pronounced hedonism, stressing the enjoyment of what life has to offer, sometimes even in excess. The noun-verb *embullo*, coined on the island, expressed the desirable experience of being swept away by the enthusiastic mood of the group. When referring to individuals who did not share this characteristic it was said (if he were a good person), *"el pobre fulano ni canta ni come fruta"* (poor soul, he doesn't sing nor eat fruit), meaning that he doesn't enjoy life. If, on the contrary, an individual was seen as selfish, humorless or antisocial, he was called a *casa sola* (alone in his house). Also, the word *sabrosa*, an adjective which literally means "tasty", achieved in Cuba, through frequent and multiple uses, the epitome of hedonistic connotation, meaning enjoyable, desirable, plentiful, and satisfying.

Cuban *novelería* (to try new things) triggered the external curiosity about other peoples' way of life as well as eagerness to adopt other languages, words, or cultural traits. *Novelería* could be interpreted as an indication of a lack of national identity. It could also be viewed as an eagerness to adopt, in an eclectic fashion, whatever is perceived as positive. This need of *estar en algo* (to be with it), *en la última* (be part of the latest fad), *no perderme nada* (to not miss anything) defines Cubans as a people for all seasons, adapting to whatever changes their accidental experience has in store. This somewhat opportunistic posture has survival value in that it readies the group for cultural borrowing: bilingualism, biculturalism, and multiculturalism.

Individualism, understood as self-worth ("I am as good as anybody else") and as a feeling of wholeness of self, was also prevalent in the Cuban culture. It has functioned to diminish the effects of any discriminatory remarks from other ethnic groups. Individualism and personalism guaranteed that any person, regardless of economic or racial background, was entitled to respect and could develop a strong ego. *Soy pobre pero honrado* (I am poor but honest) was a statement of pride in oneself which elicited social approval. Extreme individualism also supported anarchical features manifested in the national desire to do *lo que me da la gana* (what I feel like) and in the sometimes negative complacence of *Ser como soy y quiero ser* (being what I am and want to be), without much concern for the consequences.

Apparently in contradiction to individualism, but well in line with authoritarianism and personalism, were the Cuban attitudes toward leaders, which supported the loyal following of *caudillos* (strong leaders). Leaders perceived as strong personalities elicited extreme loyalty which, however, did not exempt them from criticism. Thus, Cubans did not see themselves as members of a political party or aligned with an issue but, instead, primarily as followers and friends of an individual. *Grausistas, Batistianos, Fidelistas*, were terms denoting the followers of a president or leader. Individuals, rather than institutions, elicited support.

Extreme *caudillismo* included a magical perception of political processes which was manifested in messianism. Cuba was always seen as deserving of a mystical leader who was going to bring happiness and fulfillment. Thus, people sang, *"Aquí falta señores una voz"* (There is a need for a strong voice) or *"Martí no debió de morir"* (Martí never should have died).

In addition to these generalities concerning national character and the idealization of the *campechano*, there were at least three other commonly recognized characters. Even though they were not precisely mainstream characters, they were important actors in the national drama. One was the *Guajiro* (Hick), a poor, stoic, shy, socially awkward, somewhat witty but distrustful and alineated individual, who always remained a largely unknown and marginal figure. The *Guajiros* are the people who, in retrospect, benefitted most from Castro's Revolution and who are possibly most in compliance with the system (67).

A second character was the austere, stubborn, hard working, responsible, thrifty *Gallego* (a person from the Spanish province of Galicia). The gallego was a kind-hearted, family-oriented, and friendly individual, who did not participate in Cuban hedonism and humor. The fact that these gallego qualities were attributed to all Spaniards suggests that these aspects of the Cuban character were perceived to be of Spanish origin.

The third character was the *Bicho* (trickster) (68). This very astute individual was capable of deceiving and seducing others by his wits and sense of humor. He could, and often did, get away with murder. This voluble, irresponsible opportunist would take advantage of other people's gullibility, weakness or good-heartedness. This type of person elicited some admiration in spite of his lack of integrity. These two latter counterculture characters, the *Gallego* and the *Bicho*, one exposing the socially most constructive qualities of the Cuban ethos, and the other the most antisocial qualities, were the opposing shores between which Cubans, as great sailors, navigated.

    b) National Character and Castro. Castro's revolution has greatly impacted the Cuban national character by discouraging previously admired personality traits, and fostering others which conflict with it. Thus, former virtues -personalism, individualism, flexibility, compassion, familiarity and hedonism, have become flaws; while, conversely, traits which in the past were considered flaws -*chivatear* (tattle tale), rigidity, vindictiveness, etc., have become revolutionary virtues. Revolutionary dogmatism requires critical, analytical and emotional rigidity. Since early revolutionary times, threatening slogans have expressed narrow orthodoxy such as, *"Con la Revolución o en contra"* (with the Revolution or against it), *"Patria o Muerte"* (Fatherland or death). These threatening slogans illustrate the rejection of actions illustrative of compassion, understanding and "throwing the towel" formerly characteristic of Cubans.

    The image of Cuba as an understanding, nourishing mother has been abandoned in favor of the Revolution, which is impersonal, demanding, guilt-producing, non-nourishing, and judgemental. Since the concept of the Revolution is too abstract for many to comprehend, it is important to identify the personality traits of Castro, who is its sole embodiment. The excessive cult to Castro's personality necessarily affects other people's understanding of self and their own phenomenological assessment of the Revolution. However, Castro's exalted personality can only serve as a role model for others to follow, because his characteristic behavior presupposes unlimited power.

    Castro is undoubtedly the most admired person in the island. Some of his personality traits are in line with those of other Latin *caudillos*: his daringness, unsettling maneuvers, unpredictability, fits of rage, and boisterousness, are typical qualities of the *Macho*. He is called *"El machazo de la película"* (the epitome of *machismo*). However, he lacks the more humane and personalistic traits of the *caudillo* and the *campechano* (69). Little is known of his personal life. He is not perceived as a family man: *"El no quiere ni a su madre"* (He is not capable of loving his own mother). People see him as incapable of loving a woman enough to marry her. He is, in part, responsible for the creation of this perception because of his frequent assertion that "The Revolution is my bride." He is perceived as being impartial to family and friends and incapable of compassion, because he does not forgive any misdeed: "*El no cree en nadie*" (He neither cares for anybody nor stops at anything). Castro's glimmer of generosity is expressed in an institutionalized and impersonalized manner. It is, however, demanding of public acknowledgement as expressed in that most abused sloggan, "Gracias Fidel."

The exaggerated cult to Castro's personality ascribes to him quasi-mystical characteristics among his followers. Many of the *Incondicionales* (Unconditionals) see him like a God and, through him, live and enjoy vicarious experiences of mastery and daringness. They shower him with a profane mystique as a redeemer. He is the leader who has placed Cuba on the map and "*Ha puesto a gozar a los americanos*" (He has really embarrassed the Americans). His boisterous abuse of the United States assuages inferiority feelings felt by segments of the Cuban population. These feelings had been fostered in the past by the heavy handedness of American interests in the political and economic life of the island.

Mariel informants suggest, also, that among many peasants, who constituted a large and alienated segment of the Cuban population before the Revolution, Castro's personality has even greater messianic qualities. They view Castro as a benefactor who has given their children undreamed of opportunities. Among these followers, blind and exultant feelings of loyalty are expressed, which overlook all the failings of the Revolution and the flaws of his character. The 20th century has witnessed the rise of similar charismatic leaders in instances of national ambiguity or cultural incongruency. Such leaders, like Castro, have exploited feelings of inferiority and despondence and propelled followers into unrealistic dreams of ethnic destiny. Among his followeres, however, there are also people who are not extremists and who see the Revolution in a more realistic fashion, assessing its attainments and mistakes more objectively.

Nevertheless, the cult of personality is present even among Castro's enemies, who, with admiration, describe him as a "genius for evil" and who see him as a charismatic and brilliant leader who uses his intelligence to manipulate people and situations.

Marielito informants confirm that there are many Cubans who, despite being ideologically opposed to Castro and his revolution, can respond to him, momentarily and emotionally, with fervor. During a rally such people may feel with Castro and share the fantasies of his dreams and his persuasive words of Cuba's grandeur as a revolutionary nation. Moments later, when emotions fade away, they see him and his lies for what they are.

According to informants, the majority of people either tolerate Castro or ignore him, while, nevertheless, shouting slogans at revolutionary rallies. Many feel both attraction and repulsion for his personality, which has so many common characteristics with the counter-culture *Bicho* (Trickster). The classic Bicho, through shrewdness, bold unsettling maneuvers and boastfulllness gets what he wants. Castro, the trickster, *"se las sabe todas"* (knows his ways), *"es el que más dice"* (always has the last word) and *"se mete donde le da la gana, es un fresco"* (always gets his way, because he treads where no one dares).

Castro is perceived by many as the histrionic personality who evokes collective hysterical reactions, prompted by his eloquence and, also, cues from the organizers of the rally.Others believe, however, that Castro, in most instances, is not in touch with reality, because he believes his own lies and wishful thinking. The deception is so great and widespread that there is no dialogue. The mask he wears, as well as the one worn by his followers and by all those who endure the revolution, has become permanent.

CLOSING REMARKS

It is appropriate to attempt to assess Cuba's present and future national identity in the light of the information given by the Mariel informants. This affords an opportunity to consider what the possibilities might be for the Cuban people to achieve a national identity around an ethos which would integrate the majority of the population -an ethos which would turn Cubans into actors instead of those who are acted upon-and would enable them to establish realistic and value-congruent national goals in place of mere compliance and hopeless conformity with those goals identified by the totalitarian system.

It is apparent that the Revolution's efforts to integrate the Cuban people around Communism "a la Castro" has met with dubious success. Undoubtedly Castro was unsuccessful in recruiting the former middle class, a group which had attempted to come to terms with national identity and goals. Most of the middle class has abandoned the Island (over one million).

The number of *Fidelistas* on the Island is difficult to estimate. It would be presumptuous to asume that their ranks are swelled by the totality of those large segments of the rural population who were marginal in pre-Revolutionary times or by those segments of the urban population who were alienated. It is abvious that, after 25 years of the Revolution, discontent with the system is prevalent, at least among urban dwellers of low-to-middle socio-economic background, as attested by the demographic profile of the people who left the Island during the Mariel exodus. It is also necessary to consider the possible impact that Castro's promotion of an educational infrastructure (high literacy rate, mandatory six years of schooling and broader educational opportunities for peasants) has had on this rural population (70). One informant of impoverished rural extraction, indicated that he and his high school classmates had been fervent revolutionaries. Those who went to the University started feeling uncomfortable and discontented with the lack of freedom, and absence of economic incentives and professional opportunities which Castro's Cuba offered. Therefore, it can be assumed that these people are as susceptible as the former middle class was to the attraction of the 90-mile-lure. Miami has become for Cubans on the Island a lighthouse for the discontented wrecks of Castro's communism, who see it as the promised Land of untold opportunities of freedom, experience and rewards. The Miami-Cuba axis is a very real variable when considering the destiny of the Island.

It is highly questionable that the more impassioned Fidelistas or Unconditionals, who question nothing and blindly accept everything, would be capable of integrating or assimilating whatever doctrine their unpredictable *Máximo Lider* espouses. Apparently the Revolution neither expects nor permits them to be part of the identification of national goals or the designing of the procedures to achieve them. Such blind followers are incapable of contributing anything to national identity and destiny. They are capable only of complying with the leader's whims by totally surrendering to his strong personality and political power. This interaction inhibits the development of a people's sense of self worth and feelings of self-direction.

Aside from the nominally unconditional *Incondicionales*, there are two character types which have emerged with specific personality traits and strategies that have enabled them to deal with Castro's Cuba: the opportunistic *Bicho* or *Vividor* (the trickster) and the escapist Mask. These two personality types, whose sole aspiration is to survive, are ill equipped to deal with the problems and challenges facing an underdeveloped country; —a country suffering from economic stagnation, great poppulation growth, isolation from natural markets, ostracism from many of its cultural peers in Hispanic America, as well as self-generated conflict with its powerful neighbor and former pace setter.

The Revolution has not succeeded in making Cubans identify with Third World nations and develop a new ethos according to Castro's government alignment. Informants, who had been loyal followers of Castro, over and over again, bitterly commented: "*El Tercer Mundo es un atraso, una mierda. De ahí no se saca nada*" (The Third World is backwardness, excrement. Nothing good will ever come out of it). These observations were almost always followed by some sarcastic comment about how used Cubans feel whenever Castro announces new rationing measures which are necessary because he has donated a hospital or secondary school to some "deserving" Third World country. They think that Castro's alignment with the Third World is prompted only by his personal need for glory, power and world recognition. They think that Castro is always ready to sacrifice Cuba's interests to his personal goals and to Russia's designs.

Cubans see Russia with a mixture of fear and disdain. They perceive Russian leaders as expert politicians who know what needs to be done to achieve world supremacy. However, they see ordinary Russians as robots. They call them *bolos* (bowling pins) which fall in whichever direction they are thrown. Russians are perceived as humorless, morbid people who lack social skills and cannot dance, have fun or dress well. They are resented because they are *pesados* (without wit). A popular joke says that Russians are the only people who can swim in the open ocean, because not even sharks will be interested or bothered to eat them.

In contrast, and, in spite of the official propaganda against the United States, there seems to be a growing admiration, especially among the young, for American things. American music, old American films, dances and American attire are greatly valued. Even though Americans are perceived as politically naive, they are admired as great technologists capable of scientific prowess and the producers of goods which excell those of every other nation. The America versus Russia conflict leaves Cubans very apprehensive, because they don't dare envision a world mastered by the latter. Again, the 90-mile myth and constant contact weighs heavily on the island's experience, despite political dogmatism to the contrary.

It seems impossible for Cubans, therefore, to identify with alien Third World cultures and socialist nations. If this is the case and Castro's brand of communism continues to be imposed on the island, the government has no recourse but to continue to use terrorist practices, in which they excell, to ensure compliance from large segments of the population. Thus, the Unconditionals will continue to submissively accept Castro's leadership; the tricksters will continue to marginally survive; and the Masks will continue to barely cope, without ever being capable of defining their own self identity, much less a national ethos. All of them, however, and at different times, remain susceptible to the discontent that the Miami presence so much encourages.

Despite the success of the Revolution in spreading resources in a more equitable manner; that is, turning the very poor into less poor and the middle class into poor, Castro could, conceivably, realize the economic stagnation brought about by the Revolution. This awareness, in addition to the American government's pressure and economic sanctions, could prompt him to continue to make overtures toward establishing economic and diplomatic relations with the United States.

Such a move at present is encouraged by Americans' successful curtailment of his international adventures and by Castro's hope that the lifting of the blockade would give Cuba access to more profitable markets and allow greater economic and development possibilities. If this were to happen, geopolitical and economic factors, coupled with the growth of discontent, could administer deadly blows to his totalitarian style and system.

One way or another, on the basis of the dramatic discontinuity in Cuba's cultural evolution, the value conflict between the government and the people which hinders cultural syncretism, and the emergence of personality types with weak images of self worth and little self-integrity, it must be concluded that Cubans on the island today are people who have not realized a national identity.

REFERENCES CITED

1. "Cubans vote with their feet." *Newsweek*, April 2, 1980, p. 53.
2. Nielsen, John, Rohter, Larry and Whitmore, Jane. "Nations debate ; Embassy crowds wait." *The Miami Herald*, April 10, 1980, p. 1A (Also in The cuban Exodus, Special Reprint, 1980, p.3); Martínez, Guillermo. "Thousands jam embassy in attempt to flee Cuba." *The Miami Herald*, April 7, 1980, p. 1A (Also in The Cuban Exodus, Special Reprint, 1980 p. 3).
3. Copeland, Ronald. "The Cuban boatlift of 1980: Strategies in federal crisis management." *Annals of American Academy of Political and Social Science*, May 1983, pp. 138-150.
4. "U.S. opens arms to Cuban exodus." *The Miami Herald.*, May 6, 1980, p. 1A.
5. In Spanish the ending ito (small) is added to words to denote something little and needy of protection. It is usually added to the names of children and to names denoting ethnic groups. Thus, at first the word *Marielito* had positive connotations, as opposed to *Marielero* which had a disparaging meaning.
6. During the months of January, February and March of 1980 rumors spread in Cuba concerning the impending opening of a northern port to start a boatlift similar to the one the government had begun in October, 1965, when the Camarioca port was opened. These rumors were given credibility by Castro, who in a speech on March 8, 1980, before the Third Congress of the Federation of Cuban Women, threatened: "We once had to open the Camarioca port... We feel this is proof of the lack of maturity of the U.S. government to again create similar situations." Prior to this statement he had been complaining of the alleged encouragement of the illegal departures of Cubans from the island by the U.S. government. *Gramma Weekly Summary*, March 16, 1980, p. 4.; "C.I.A.: Castro usa éxodo para refrenar descontento." *El Miami Herald*, Dec. 29, 1980, p. 6A.
7. It is interesting to notice that Castro admitted that there are still "antisocial" elements in Cuba despite his earlier claims that the Revolution had eliminated all traces of prostitution, gambling, and the like.
8. Personal communication. Friends of the author chartered a boat to pick up several relatives residing on the island. Among

them were a son who was an engineer, his wife and their children. When the person who chartered the boat arrived in Mariel, he was told that his son could not leave, because he was a professional who owed his career to the Revolution; his wife and children, falling in the category of "scum," could leave. Negotiations started between the father and Cuban authorities regading the amount of money that the government would take in exchange for his son. He offered $4,000 which was all the cash he had, and, as they refused the offer, he had to leave with the daughter-in-law and the grandchildren but without the son. Later, in Miami, the father approached Castro's agents, who offered to get his son an exit permit if he would give them $15,000. Negotiations were fruitful and the son was allowed to leave through Costa Rica. This odyssey cost that family over $30,000 in expenses (chartering the boat, ransom price, passage and stay in Costa Rica, etc.).

9. "F.B.I. discovers some undesirables among flood of refugees from Cuba." *The Washington Post*, April 29, 1980, p. 1A.; "Some refugees suffer psychological problems." *The Miami Herald*, May 1, 1980, p. 16A.; "Three cases of leprosy." *The Miami Herald*, May 17, 1980, p. 1C.; "Little Havana attacked by boatlift criminals." *The Miami Herald*, Sept. 18, 1980, p. 1A.; Michelmore, Peter. "From Cuba with hate." *Readers Digest*, Dec., 1982, pp. 221-248.

10. The City of Miami, in an effort to solve the housing problems of the refugees and to facilitate service delivery, built a tent city under Expressway I-95 in the area East of Little Havana. See "Tent city will fold within month." *The Miami Herald*, Sept. 3, 1980.

11. Mental health professionals who came via Mariel had difficulties in dealing with sociopaths. They did not perceive them as mental patients in need of treatment but as socially maladjusted persons who deserved punishment. In many instances the treatment modality they used was designed to help clients cope instead of aiding them to gain some insight into their problems. When dealing with homosexuals they helped the client devise strategies to deceive others about their sexual preference instead of supporting them in their process of self acceptance. Furthermore, they tended to be very authoritarian and direct with their clients, which was not conducive to encouraging

them to be a part of the therapeutic process.

12. Nineteen key informants were reinterviewed. The information obtained was very consistent with what they had reported before. There were changes, however, in the way they interpreted life in the U.S.A. Many had come to terms with reality and the need to keep a job and save in order to survive. They reported that life here was hard, and complained about the cost of education and health services. However, they felt that coming to the U.S.A., despite shattered, unrealistic expectattions, was the most positive decision they had made in their lives.

13. Bach, Robert L. "The new Cuban immigrants: Their background and prospects." *Monthly Labor Review*, Oct., 1980, pp. 39-46.

14. Clark, Juan M. "The 1980 Mariel exodus: An assessment and prospect." Unpublished monograph, n.d.

15. Ibid. See Table 2, page 81a.

16. Bach, op. cit., pp. 44-45.

17. Williams, Dan. "One family: In Havana, they cower from wrath of neighbors". *The Miami Herald*, April 22, 1980, p. 1A (Also in The Cuban Exodus, Special Reprint, 1980, p. 5); "Obligan a una cubana a recorrer las calles de la Habana con un cartel infamante colgado al cuello." *Diario de las Américas*, Mayo 22, 1980, p. 10.; "Mini-rallies jeer Cubans waiting to join exodus." *The Miami Herald*, May 23, 1980, p. 24A. The author's nephew was attacked by a mob when he attempted to enter the Peruvian Embassy. They broke one of his teeth. The home of the author's uncle was assaulted twice while he waited to obtain the exit permit.

18. Evidence is abundant of the abuses experienced by mental patients who were shipped in boats without concern for their safety. See "Some refugees suffer psychological problems." *The Miami Herald*, May 1980, p. 16A. In October, 1980, the American Psychiatric Association expressed its concern about the inhuman treatment given to hospitalized mental patients who were sent in the flotilla without consideration for them or their relatives.

19. Clark, Juan M. and Figueras, Juan A. *Totalitarian Repression in Cuba*. Unpublished monograph, n.d., pp. 49-51.

20. Ibid., p. 1.

21. Ibid., p. 4. For more information on this subject see Clark, Juan M. and Figueras, Juan A. *Cuba's Totalitarian Economy*. Unpublished monograph. See also *Resumen de Entrevistas con Cubanos*. Miami: Agrupación Abdala, 1979-80.

22. "Life in Cuba today." In "The Cubans, a people changed, Special Report." *The Miami Herald*, Dec. 18, 1983, p. 12M.

23. Ibid.

24. Recarte, Alberto. *Cuba: Economía y Poder (1959-1980*. Madrid: Alianza Editorial, 1980, p. 116.

25. A 25-year-old male former student of architecture at the University of Havana informed the author that a graduate thesis presented there in 1980 dealt with the office space needs of the new local government *Poder Popular* (Popular Power) and how to adapt houses to those needs.

26. A 23-year-old male informant reported that one of the worst slums is *Palo Cagado* (Shitty Stick) in Mariano, Havana.

27. Another informant reported that the housing development in Alamar is in shambles because of the use of inferior construction materials.

28. According to informants, in parts of Havana, the *aguateros* (water people) make a living selling water.

29. According to an informant, the Ration Book is "the sword of Democles," hanging over the head of every single Cuban, since, if by any reason, like in the Padilla case, one is deprived of it, one is condemned to starvation.

30. The quantity of food allotted to people living outside of the capital is even less. Chicken and meat are alternated according to availability.

31. Carlos Ripol in his article, *"En defensa de un marxista"* (In defense of a Marxist) published in *El Miami Herald*, argues that alienation from the system and questioning of it is growing among those segments of the population who has had access to education for the first time. Later, in this article, the author makes reference to this situation based on information given by three informants of peasant background. On the other hand, the government has failed to graduate enough technicians while there has been an excess of graduates in other fields who are now suffering from unemployment or underemployment.

32. The informant said that old Charles Chaplin movies depicting

abject poverty in the U.S.A. as well as documentaries made during the struggles of the civil rights movement are used out of context by Castro's government to perpetuate negative images of the United States. Another informant mentioned the documentary film called "Now," produced by the ICAIC at Havana University in the mid-1960's, which deals with the abuses of black people in the U.S.A. prior to the civil rights movement. They show the films as if conditions had not changed.

33. "Millares solicitan asistencia a Esatdos Unidos para salir de Cuba." *El Miami Herald*, Dec. 16, 1980, p. 5. See also Clark, Juan M. "The 1980 Mariel Exodus: An Assessment and Prospect." Unpublished monograph. Clark reports that unpublished records of the Comité de Planificación de Población of the Central Planning Board of Cuba show that by June, 1980, 1,285,000 persons had applied to leave. By the end of Dec., 1980, the U.S. Interest Section in Havana had received 130,000 letters representing over 600,000 people.

34. The psychiatrists who worked under the author's direction confirmed that, in Cuba, physicians grant medical certificates to friends and *socios* to excuse their absences from jobs and revolutionary meetings.

35. According to the yearbook published by the United Nations in 1978 (pp. 431-433), Cuba is suffering from one of the highest divorce rates in the world.

36. Sandoval, Mercedes C. "Santería." *Journal of the Florida Medical Association*, Vol 70, No. 8, August, 1983, p. 628.

37. Sandoval, Mercedes Cros. *La Religión Afrocubana*. Madrid: Editorial Playor, 1975. See also Sandoval, Mercedes C. "Afrocuban concepts of disease and its treatment in Miami." *Journal of Operational Psychiatry*, Vol. 8, No. 2, 1977, pp. 52-63; Sandoval, Mercedes C. "Santería as a mental health care system." *Social Science and Medicine*, Vol. 13B, No. 2, 1979, pp. 137-151.

38. Ibid.; Halifax, Joan and Weidman, Hazel. "Religion as a mediating institution in acculturation: The case of Santería y Greater Miami." In Cox, Richard H. (Ed.), *Religious Systems and Psychotherapy*. Springfield, Ill: Charles C. Thomas, 1973, pp. 319-331.

39. For more information on this subject see Clark, Juan M. and Figueras, Juan A. *Totalitarian Repression in Cuba*. Unpublis-

hed monograph.

40. Balmaseda, Liz. "Return to Puerto Padre, my hometown: A place I never knew." In "The Cubans, a people changed, Special Report." *The Miami Herald*, Dec. 18, 1983, p. 23M.

41. Under the term, "improper conduct" the government lumps any behavior which it considers dangerous, antirevolutionary and punishable even if it doesn't involve an infraction of the law. During a film festival celebrated in Miami in February, 1984, an investigative film by Nestor Almendros and Orlando Real was shown. It depicted the repression of homosexuals in Cuba. In this regard it is interesting to note how selective discrimination and the term "improper conduct" is applied in Cuba according to Revolutionary whims or designs. Persecution of homosexuals in Cuba has been characterized by lack of consistency. According to informants, there are the *Maricones Sagrados* (sacret fags) who are intellectuals or artists partial to the Revolution and who enjoy all types of honors, recognition and advantages. They are sent to congresses and cultural events all over the world. Then there are the *Maricones Serios* (serious Homosexuals) who are those homosexals who exhibit behavior which does not portray their sexual preferences. These individuals are not bothered by the regime. The *Locas* (drag queens), whose public behavior is highly conspicuous and effeminate, are the ones who have been persecuted, physically and psychologically abused and, in some instances, placed in concentration camps (UMAP) or shipped out through Mariel. This could mean that the regime cannot tolerate the existence on the island of people who dare "lift their mask" and act according to their preferences, sexual or otherwise.

42. Lumpen is a word used to refer to those people who, according to the socialist regime, live off the work of others; people who don't produce anything. Lumpen-proletariat, according to Marx and Engels, are a dangerous class, the social scum. See Marx, Karl and Engels, Friederich. *The Communist Manifesto*. New York: International Publisher, 1948, p.20.

43. During 1975 *Gramma* newspaper published a series of articles against "bolas" or rumors which they felt were alarming and harmful.

44. Alvarez Díaz, J., Arredondo, A., Shelton, R.M. and Vizcaíno, J. *Cuba Geopolítica y Pensamiento Económico*. Miami: Cole-

gio de Economistas de Cuba en el Exilio, 1964, pp. 35-41.

45. On the origins of Cuban culture see: Pittaluga, Gustavo. *Diálogo Sobre el Destino*. Memosyne, 1969 (originally published in 1954); Lizaso, Felix. *Panorama de la Cultura Cubana*. México: Fondo de Cultura Económica, 1948; Vitier, Medardo. *Las Ideas en Cuba*. La Habana: Editorial Trópico, 1938; Vitier, Medardo. *La Filosofía en Cuba*. México: Fondo de Cultura Económica, 1948.

46. Ortíz, Fernando. "La hija cubana del iluminismo." *Revista Bimestre Cubana*, Vol. 2, No. 1, p. 12.

47. Ortíz Fernández, Fernando. *Contrapunteo Cubano del Tabaco y el Azucar*. Caracas: Biblioteca Aguerecho, 1978.

48. Vitier, M. Las Ideas en Cuba, op. cit.

49. Portell Vilá, Herminio. *Historia de Cuba en sus Relaciones con Estados Unidos y España*. Habana: Jesús Montero, 1938-1941 (4 Vols.).

50. Ibid.

51. Alvarez Díaz, J. et al., op. cit., p. 172.

52. Jenks, Leland H. *Our Cuban Colony*. New York: Vanguard Press, 1928.

53. Alvarez Díaz, J. et al., op. cit., pp. 365-374.

54. For a detailed treatment of this subject see Klein, Herbert S. *Slavery in the Americas: A Comparative Study of Virginia and Cuba*. Chicago: University of Chicago Press, 1967. See also Hanke, Lewis. *The Spanish Struggle for Justice in the Conquest of America*. Boston: Little and Brown, 1965.

55. *Un Estudio Sobre Cuba: Colonia, República, Experimento Socialista*. Miami: Grupo Cubano de Investigaciones Económicas de University of Miami, 1963, pp. 781-1277.

56. Schroeder, Susan. *Cuba: A Handbook of Historical Statistics*. G.K. Hall, 1982, p. 125.

57. Alvarez Díaz, J. et al., op. cit., pp. 375-424.

58. Kluckhohn, Florence R. and Strodbeck, F.L. *Variations in Value Orientations*. New York: Row, Peterson and Co., 1961.

59. Weidman, Hazel H. and collaborators. *The Miami Health Ecology Project Report, Vol. I*. Miami: University of Miami School of Medicine, 1978.

60. Sandoval, Mercedes C. "El ethos cubano." *Krisis*, Vol. 1, No. 4, 1976, pp. 18-20, 28, 30.

61. Egeland, Janice. *The Miami Health Ecology Project Report,*

Vol II: The Value Orientation Study. Miami: University of Miami School of Medicine, 1976.

62. Ibid., pp. 121-127.

63. Ibid., pp. 128-135.

64. Ibid., pp. 114-121.

65. Ibid., pp. 136-142.

66. For more information on the Cuban character see: Sandoval, M.C. "El ethos cubano," op. cit.; "El caso de la embajada del Perú y el Mariel." *Reencuentro Cubano*, 1981, pp. 26-27. 67.

67. In 1959 many rural areas in Cuba were still isolated despite the fact that over 45% of the total population was rural. Today, isolation is still prevalent and living conditions are far from satisfactory. However, public education and health services have, indeed, reached these marginal areas.

68. There is documentation in the Spanish literature of a counter-culture *picaresco* (trickster) tradition in Spain tracing back to the fifteenth century. These are transient, alienated people who get their way by deception and daring and who always skirt the law.

69. Castro keeps his private life away from the public eye. However, much has been written about the way in which his early life experiences, his turbulent family background, his unhappy childhood and adolescence, etc., affected his character. See Alvarez Díaz, J., op. cit., pp. 456-488.

70. This is important in the light of a trend that has continued into the Revolutionary period, whereby peasants move into urban areas. According to Susan Schroeder (op. cit., p. 56), the urban population has grown from 52.1% in 1960 to 64.4% in 1980. Estimates for the year 2,000 are that it will reach 73.3%.

CONTENTS